REALIZING
THE
SELF
WITHIN

Expressing Your Spiritual Self
in Everyday Life

by SUE PRESCOTT

E

Elfin Cove Press
Seattle, Washington

ELFIN COVE PRESS
1481 130th Ave. NE
Bellevue, WA 98005
www.elfincovepress.com

Project manager: Bernie Kuntz
Cover design: Ken Susynski
Cover photograph: Helge Pedersen
Text design: Laurel Strand

Library of Congress 99-072914

ISBN 0944958-49-4

291.4

Printed in the United States of America
3   5   7   9   10   8   6   4   2

Table of Contents

Introduction

The desire for self-improvement can be found among all people. *Realizing the Self Within* is designed with that in mind. My goal in writing this book is to explain, in easy-to-understand language, the concepts of spirituality and what it means to be Self-realized. I hope to illustrate how you can use this knowledge in a practical manner to improve relationships and make your life happier and more fulfilled.

Realizing the Self Within is structured in the form of a seven-week class, with each chapter describing a different class session. Speaking to a fictional group of students allows me to make the information clear and easy to grasp, yet more interesting because of their questions and comments about the material.

The information presented in this book does not originate with me. It has been synthesized from the teachings of various spiritual leaders, as well as from the traditional religions of the world. I have also included quotes from poets, psychologists, philosophers, and scientists to help you understand the subject more completely.

Realizing the Self Within provides a basis from which you can branch out as you undertake your own personal exploration of spirituality and its meaning in your life.

Sue Prescott

The Planes of Consciousness

As I greeted the people entering my class on "Self-Realization in Everyday Life," I was full of excitement and anticipation. I looked forward to teaching them how the concepts of spirituality were relevant to their lives.

During my own spiritual search, one of the questions I pondered was whether the knowledge of spirituality could be helpful during times of stress. Could it be applied when you get into an argument with someone? Would it be helpful when you suffer a major disappointment?

A central theme of my class is learning to become more in tune with your "Higher Self," or, as I call it, your spiritual Self. This is the Self within. When you do this, remarkable changes occur. To put it simply, you learn to be a better person.

For example, you learn to see yourself more objectively and to analyze why you do things you regret. You gain insight into how to change personality qualities that you don't like. You also widen your sense of self and learn not to be so hard on yourself. You realize you are in a continuous process of learning, which includes making mistakes.

What constitutes your self-esteem also changes. You let go of your reliance on physical characteristics to define yourself, such as your hairstyle, size, or style of dress. You realize you don't need to base your sense of worth on these attributes. Your self-concept expands to incorporate aspects of your inner spirituality, rather than rely on your personality and physical body. You learn to accept yourself more thoroughly, because at the level of your "Higher Self," you are not lacking or incomplete.

At the start of any class I teach, I let the participants know that time will be allotted for discussion and personal reflection. I encourage people to share as much as they feel comfortable, while emphasizing that they will not be pressured to speak. Anyone can choose not to join the exercises done in class. If they wish, they may merely observe.

I have an introductory exercise that I like to do to launch the first session. Instead of just going around the room and having people share a few remarks about themselves, this exercise has a twist to it that makes it more fun. It helps remove some of the tension people feel when talking in front of strangers.

In the exercise, each person lights a match and holds it as it burns down. You tell as much as you can about yourself — but only while the match is burning. When you have to blow out the match so you won't get burned, your turn is over.

I reminded everyone they can "pass" on the exercise if they feel uncomfortable. If they prefer, they can say a few things about themselves without holding a match.

I lit a match and began. "I'm Sue. I am a social worker. I do family, marital, and individual therapy. I have three children. Two are in college, and one son is still at home. We live in a condo in Kirkland. I play soccer, take ballet lessons, and participate in a few meditation groups."

When I finished, I passed the matches to the next person, a former client of mine named Jim. Privately, I was relieved because I knew he would probably do the exercise without feeling intimidated. He would be a model for others in the group.

Jim lit the match and said, "My name is Jim. This is my wife, Anne. I am a manager at Star Computing. My background is in business and computers. We have two teenage daughters. I enjoy doing things with the family, such as boating and snow skiing. I also love to read."

Jim gave the matches to Anne, who nervously lit one. She said, "I'm Anne. As Jim said, we are married. We have two girls still at home. I am a homemaker now. Long ago, I taught kindergarten. I enjoy doing things with my daughters and am active in the school PTSA." She blew out her match and handed the matches to the next person.

This was Jane, another client I had seen in the past. She said that she worked in data entry at a local manufacturing company and that she was single, having divorced several years earlier. She shared that she had come in for therapy with me during her divorce and often attended classes I led. She concluded by saying she had two grown children and liked gardening, reading, and spending time with her granddaughter.

Jane passed the matches to the person next to her, a woman named Lisa. Lisa said she was a teacher and had recently remarried a man who traveled two or three days every week. She thought the class sounded interesting and had free time to take it because her husband was out of town. She was raised Catholic, but hadn't gone to church in years.

Al, a man in his sixties, related that his wife was the organist for their church and played for choir practice the same evening the class took place. He dropped her off at the church on his way to the class. Al was an active member of his church and had studied quite a lot about other religions. He said he was eager to learn about the concepts I planned to cover in the class and was hoping to pass on the information to other members of his church.

One other couple had yet to introduce themselves. The husband reluctantly took out a match.

"I'm not very good at this type of thing," he said. "My name is Don. I heard about the class from my wife, who said we needed to do more things together. I agreed to come in exchange for her agreeing to let me join a bowling league."

The class laughed, and Don quickly added, "I also thought it would do me some good. I'm in construction and have two grown kids."

The last person to speak lit a match and said, "I'm Laura, and I'm married to Don. The minute I read about this class, I wanted to attend. I am always reading books and magazine articles about spirituality and have a lot of time on my hands now that our children are grown."

THE NATURE OF CONSCIOUSNESS

"What I plan to teach you in this class harmonizes with traditional religion," I began. "All religions share the same fundamental truths, such as the awareness of a spiritual essence within each person and the acknowledgment of an underlying unity existing in all of life. These truths are part of what is called the 'Ancient Wisdom.' This is the body of knowledge about spirituality that has been handed down throughout the ages. It has been taught by the Egyptians, the Babylonians, the ancient Greeks through their Mystery Schools, the Jews through the Kabbalah, Plato, Socrates, the Chinese, the Mayans, and the Native Americans. This list is not complete, but it gives you an idea of the universality of the information.

"Because spirituality is not physical or visible, many of the teachings have been given in myths, parables, or symbols to communicate their meaning. This has been found to be the case on every continent and in every tribe or culture. During this class, I will often use some of these stories to illustrate the concept we're discussing.

"One point I want to emphasize to you is to listen to everything I say with a discerning mind. Analyze it and reason it through. My purpose is not to have you unquestioningly accept and believe the ideas I introduce. Rather, I want you to listen with an open mind and simply understand what is being presented. Then test it out with your own thinking and see if it rings true with your inner perceptions and intuition.

"One of my teachers used to say repeatedly, 'As the Buddha said, "Believe nothing! Not by any authority. If what is being said seems to you to be reasonable and logical, try it on as a *theory*, until you know it to be true." '

"I encourage you to feel free to interrupt me at any time with questions or comments. I welcome input in this way because the discussion that follows will help clarify the topic.

"I'd like to begin my presentation tonight by talking about the concept of consciousness. You have probably all heard the term. But what does it mean? What does it refer to? To help you understand it more thoroughly, I'll ask you some questions so you can identify it for yourself.

"First of all, how do you know you are alive?"

There was silence in the room before Jim volunteered, "Because I feel my body. I can hear my heart beat and feel my breathing. I know I exist because I am here. There is a distinct *feeling* that I exist."

Lisa offered, "I know I exist because I am aware of it. I am aware of how I feel. I'm aware that time goes by. A combination of things lets me know I am alive."

I looked at Anne and asked what she thought. After a brief hesitation, she replied, "I just know I exist. I can't explain how I know, but I do."

"All these answers relate to your sense of being," I said. "You are aware of being inside and using your body. You experience changeable feelings and moods. You know what you think and how it is to reason. Each one of these contributes to the recognition that you are alive.

"The sense of knowing you exist is more immediate than thought. It is within you all the time, whether you are happy or sad, old or young.

"Being aware of yourself is the same as being *conscious* of yourself. You are conscious of having a body and moving it wherever you want to go. You are conscious of experiencing feelings and thoughts. The part of you that is aware of all this is the sense of 'I.' The 'I' provides a label for your consciousness.

"Awareness of yourself is with you all the time. You are even aware of yourself when you dream, although you don't feel the sensation of being inside your body at that time."

At this point, I distributed a handout and opened a large tablet listing the different levels of consciousness. I explained we would be discussing them in more detail later on, but I wanted to introduce them briefly.

LEVELS OF CONSCIOUSNESS

Personal Self   Physical Body and Body Mind
                Emotional Body
                Lower Mental Body — *This is the everyday mind.*
Spiritual Self   Higher Mental Body — *This is the part of the mind that receives intuition and utilizes reason and wisdom.*
                Intuitional Body
                Field of Unity

"Your consciousness exists on several levels within you, ranging from body awareness to spiritual insight," I said. "You can be aware of any of these levels at any one point in time. Let me explain what I mean.

"First of all, you live in the world using your physical body. This is the lowest level of consciousness. You experience life through your senses. You see, hear, feel hunger, and know when you are moving. Knowledge of the physical plane of existence is communicated through your five senses of sight, smell, taste, touch, and hearing.

"Some of your body's functions are automatic, such as breathing or digestion, and others are done by choice, such as when you decide to walk from one place to another.

"For the automatic functions, the body has a 'mind of its own' so you don't have to remember to make your heart beat or your organs function. This automatic 'mind' is evident in your reflexes. If you touch a hot iron, your arm automatically pulls your hand away. This happens faster than it would if you had to think about it. This is the autonomic nervous system, or what is also called 'the body mind.' "

Lisa said, "I know what you mean by the body having a mind of its own. When I get startled, I jump up and down and almost run in place. It must be a reaction in case I really needed to run away from something."

"That's right," I said. "The body mind is very protective. It keeps up the muscle tone in your body so you can react quickly if you are startled or in danger. The job of the body mind is to take care of your physical body and keep it healthy.

"The next level of consciousness is that of your emotions. When you feel love, sympathy, nervousness, or anger, you are functioning at the emotional level. Wants and desires are also experienced here.

"After the emotional body comes the mental body — your mind. At the mental level, you think your thoughts. You plan, solve problems, and weigh factors to make decisions.

"Your mind works closely with your emotional body. It takes the messages from your emotions, such as dislike, and makes plans and decisions so you will feel better. For example, while being seated in a restaurant, you may feel uncomfortable in one area — which is an emotional response — and make a decision — which is a mental function — to sit elsewhere.

"Again, I want to emphasize that your consciousness operates at many levels at once. For example, on the physical level, you may be aware your stomach feels full from an evening meal. On the emotional level, you are happy anticipating going to a movie. At the same time, your mental body may prompt you to look up the time the theater will show the movie and plan when you need to leave home.

"There is also an aspect of your mind that is open to moments of insight and intuition. This is different from your normal, everyday mind. It is referred to as 'the higher mind.' It is the part of your mind that links with your intuition. You use it when you reason something through or think in the abstract.

"The higher mind also hears messages from your conscience. It is the part of you that knows right from wrong. You might choose the 'wrong' action in any set of circumstances, but your higher mind tells you it isn't right. The higher mind gives you knowledge of fairness and justice.

"The next level of consciousness is your intuitional body. When you are able to tap into your insight or intuition, this is the part of your consciousness you access.

"You aren't open to this level very often. Your everyday mind occupies you so completely that the information from the intuitional plane generally doesn't come through. Sometimes insights are picked up while you are asleep and dreaming. The inspiration for great painters and poets comes from this field.

"The term 'field' is used to indicate these different levels of consciousness. The intuitional body can also be called the intuitional field. You may have heard the word used to describe the magnetic field surrounding high-voltage power lines.

"The highest level of consciousness is the field of Unity. Each of us is connected to this field simply by being alive. This is the plane or field from which everything in our world emerges. This includes our planet, the solar system, and the entire universe.

"Your consciousness doesn't operate at this level when you are living in a physical body, however. You can only sense it intuitively because it is beyond anything physical, emotional, or mental. It is the ultimate of spirit. It is Unity itself."

Al spoke up, "It sounds like this is what Christians call 'God.' "

"Yes, the field of Unity is also called God, the Supreme, the Divine Spirit, or the God plane," I said. "Each person, animal, and object is a creation of the Universal Spirit and has this essence within.

"The term 'spirituality' comes from the Latin word for 'breath.' This refers to the One Breath from which all arises. This symbolizes the Oneness of all. The spirit in each of us is our connection to the field of Unity. It is also our connection to everything else.

"You utilize and express all the levels of consciousness as you participate in the events of your life. Let me give an example.

"While standing in line at a supermarket to buy your food, you feel a push and a bump on your back — the physical level. You feel irritated about the collision — the emotional level — and turn around to see the person who ran into you. As you see the elderly gentleman who lost his balance — the mental level — you understand he ran into you by accident — the intuitional level. You reach out to help him and see if he is again steady on his feet. As your feelings turn to compassion and helpfulness, you smile and say you hope he is okay — the field of Unity.

"Each level of consciousness is an aspect of a human being and not a separate and distinct thing. All levels together make the whole. Let me show you a demonstration that illustrates this point."

I explained to the class that, whenever I teach a concept, I like to use visual aids and hands-on examples. The objects I brought this evening were a prism and a flashlight. I dimmed the lights and directed the beam from the flashlight into the crystal. All the colors of the rainbow were projected onto the wall.

"You can see how the crystal disperses ordinary white light into the color spectrum of red, orange, yellow, green, blue, indigo, and violet," I said. "Notice how one color gradually changes into the next.

"The same is true with the levels of consciousness. One level gradually changes into the next. All the levels together make up a human being.

"These levels of consciousness are also called 'planes' of consciousness. I'd like to explain how different the higher planes of consciousness are from the lower by referring to them as different dimensions."

I held up a page of notebook paper.

"The surface of this piece of paper can be said to be two-dimensional, with a width of eight-and-a-half inches and a length of eleven inches."

Using the same piece of paper, I folded it into the shape of a box. "If you add another dimension to length and width, you get height. This forms a box, which is three-dimensional.

"The physical body can be said to be three-dimensional. So are all the things in the world that can be seen and touched, including the Earth itself.

"This is the physical plane of consciousness.

"Since the level of consciousness of the physical body is three-dimensional, or 3-D, if you add another dimension to it by including your emotions, it can be said to be 4-D. This adds an entirely new component to your consciousness.

"Think of how different your emotions are from your body. The emotional plane doesn't have length, width, or depth. It has nothing to do with space. Your emotions transcend, or move beyond, space, as well as time.

"Moving to the next plane of consciousness, which is the mind, you can think of it as the fifth dimension. Again, notice the vast difference between how you feel and how you think.

"Above that plane is the sixth dimension, which is the intuitional plane.

"Finally, the seventh dimensional plane is the field of Unity. You may have heard the expression 'Seventh Heaven,' which is used to describe something that is so wonderful it can hardly be expressed. The field of Unity is beyond description and you can only begin to grasp it through your intuition."

Al raised a question. "When you say 'higher' planes of consciousness, are they higher *in* the body, or higher *than* the body?"

"The higher levels of consciousness are not necessarily higher in the body or above the body," I replied. "The higher planes of consciousness exist *within* the body. The term 'higher' is used because it refers to the higher or faster rate of vibration of the energy at the higher planes.

"This is similar to the various wavelengths of the colors that make a rainbow. Red is the color at one end of the visible spectrum and violet is at the other. Red has the longest wavelength and lowest frequency, or cycles per second, and violet has the highest. The same comparison can be made to the planes of consciousness. The physical body has the slowest rate of vibration while the intuitional body has the fastest.

"In turn, within each plane of consciousness, there is a range of vibrations. For example, on the emotional plane, happy feelings vibrate faster than sad feelings, such as grief or sorrow. Painful emotions are dense and heavy, as in the expression 'heavy with sorrow.' When you are depressed, the expression 'I feel low' refers to the low level of vibration of this emotional state. Your level of physical energy is also low when you feel this way. You feel tired because you have a low level of vitality."

I stopped my talk and took out two bells. One was very small and the other was about four times larger. "I'd like to demonstrate how the various levels of consciousness can vibrate together within a human being. If I ring this larger bell, it has a fairly low sound."

I rang the bell and let its sound ring out for a few moments. After setting it down, I picked up the smaller bell and rang it. "You can tell by the higher pitch of this bell that the sound vibrations are moving at a faster rate than the larger bell."

I then rang the two bells together. Both sounds could be heard. "This is like the many rates of vibration of energy within you. They all vibrate together. It illustrates how you can have more than one feeling at once. It also shows how you can be thinking everyday thoughts and have a flash of intuition at the same time.

"Relating back to your question, Al, there is another reason why the word 'higher' — as in higher consciousness — has the connotation of being physically higher than the body. That is because of the concept of heaven.

"Heaven is thought of as being up in the sky. One reason for this is when you look at the sky, you see a vastness that appears to have no end. Heaven seems to be as limitless and widespread as the sky. The highest levels of consciousness are like 'heaven,' with qualities that are inconceivable."

Jim spoke up. "I noticed you used the word 'body' when you described the different levels of consciousness. Can you explain what you mean by the emotional body, for instance? Why is it called a body?"

"The term 'body' can be thought of as a 'part' or 'component,' as in 'emotional component,' " I answered. "The word 'vehicle' is also used in describing any of the levels of consciousness."

"The physical body can be thought of as the 'physical vehicle,' just as the emotional body can be referred to as the 'emotional vehicle.' Your spiritual Self uses the physical and emotional bodies as vehicles in which it can exist on the physical plane, or our planet Earth.

"Also, each vehicle or body has a different function from the rest, even though they gradually transition from one into the other."

Lisa asked, "So what is the Higher Self?"

"I refer to the Higher Self as your 'spiritual Self,' " I said. "I don't really like the term 'Higher Self,' because it has a connotation of being physically higher and separate from your body. Your Higher Self, or spiritual Self, is as much a part of you as your physical body is.

"Your spiritual Self is composed of your higher mental body, your intuitional body, and your connection to the field of Unity. Many different words refer to it. You probably have heard of the term 'soul.' That is the spiritual Self. One of my teachers referred to it as the 'Inner Self.' Others simply call it the 'Self,' with a capital 'S.'

"I prefer to use the term 'spiritual Self.' This makes it easily understood. I don't want to repeatedly say the 'capital "S" Self' or the 'lowercase "s" self' when I refer to them. When I speak of the 'spiritual Self,' I am making a clear distinction from the everyday self. We will discuss the spiritual Self in depth during a later class.

"So this can all sink in a bit, let's take a break. It is a lot to absorb."

MEDITATION AND BREATHING EXERCISES

"Before we continue our discussion of the personal self, I'd like to lead you through a brief meditation.

"There are many kinds of meditation, with various procedures and different goals. Meditation can range from simple relaxation exercises designed to ease the tension of your physical body to deeply spiritual disciplines.

"During each class, we will try out a different type of meditation. Since you are just beginning, I plan to start you out with a simple meditation focusing on relaxation and breathing techniques.

"Initially, I'd like to have you stretch a bit. Stand and spread apart so you can reach your hands above your head and bend over freely, without hitting anyone."

Everyone in the class followed my directions, but some did so only hesitantly. Don voiced his apprehension by commenting, "I don't know about doing a lot of bending and stretching. I'm no 'spring chicken.' "

"Do what you can," I said. "Take it slowly and gradually. It doesn't matter how far you can reach. The reason we are doing this is to get your energy circulating freely.

"First of all, stretch your hands over your head and reach toward the ceiling. Reach as high as you can with the fingers of your hands outstretched. Look up as you reach and grab the air four times.

"Bend over and touch the floor or as far down as you can go. Extend your arms fully and gently stretch your back out for four counts. Let your head and arms hang loosely as you remain bent at the waist. Allow your shoulders and neck to loosen.

"Slowly raise yourself up, and as you do so, inhale deeply. Allow yourself to feel a sense of relaxation.

"Now, alternately roll your shoulders in a large circle. Start with the right shoulder and then the left.

"Next, move your awareness up to your neck muscles and let them relax. Rotate your head gently and slowly in a wide circle, releasing any muscle tension you find. Rotate once clockwise and then counterclockwise. Repeat this a few times."

As Anne was doing the bending and stretching, she felt self-conscious. She looked at Jim, who was doing the exercises wholeheartedly. She caught his eye and he winked at her. She felt encouraged and continued to stretch. A few people groaned as they bent over to touch their toes. Anne was glad she could do this without difficulty.

"Let's take our seats now so we can do some breathing exercises," I said.

"Close your eyes, relax your body, and release any left-over tension in your stomach, neck, and shoulders.

"Take a few deep, cleansing breaths. Inhale deeply, then fully exhale, letting all the air out of your lungs. As you breathe in again, relax your body even more with your next exhalation.

"Take full, deep breaths through your nose so the sound of your inhalation can be heard. Exhale slowly and deliberately by blowing out the air through semi-closed lips.

"After two or three cleansing breaths, breathe normally, letting the relaxation spread throughout your entire body. Take a few moments to settle into a regular breathing pattern.

"As we begin the first breathing technique, on your inhaling breath, count it silently to yourself as 'one.'

"As you exhale, count 'two.'

"Inhale again and count this breath as 'three.' Continue until you reach ten. Then start again with 'one' on the next inhalation. Continue for awhile with this pattern as you allow your relaxation to deepen."

I paused so people could practice this breathing pattern and experience its benefits. After a few minutes, I said, "Let's try another type of breathing. Continue to be aware of your breath and as you inhale, mentally say to yourself the word 'in.' As you exhale, mentally say the word 'out.' Repeat this technique for a few minutes."

I watched the class do the breathing exercise and could see several people mouthing the words "in" and "out." I noticed a few people who looked fairly relaxed in their shoulders, but several others still seemed pretty tense.

"Let's shift to another breathing technique. This time as you breathe, pause for a moment at the top of your inhalation. Then let yourself exhale. At the lowest point of your exhalation, pause once again. Repeat this pattern for a few minutes."

As I did the exercise with the class, I recalled how much I like this particular breathing method. The pause is very effective in helping me detach from my regular thinking and relax my body and mind.

I brought the meditation to a close, and when everyone had opened their eyes, I asked, "What did you think about the exercise?"

A few people said they found the breathing exercises soothing and relaxing.

"Did you find your mind wandering during the meditation?" I asked. Some nodded.

Al said, "I couldn't believe how hard it was to focus on my breathing. It seemed to be only a few seconds before I was off in a reverie."

Don laughed and said, "I couldn't concentrate either. I've got too many things on my mind!"

"I know what you mean, Don," I said. "That's why concentrating on a breathing pattern can help. Otherwise, your mind runs free and flits like a butterfly from one thought to the next. Because of the mind's constantly changing nature, it has been referred to as the 'monkey mind' as it swings from one topic to another. Another name for the constant train of thoughts is 'mind noise.'

"It is difficult to shut off your thinking and quiet your mind. But in order to meditate deeply, you need to develop this skill. That's why I started you out with breathing techniques. They give you something to focus on as you gain control over your thoughts.

"If you find your mind wandering when you try to meditate, return to your favorite breathing pattern. It provides you with a way to clear your mind once again. Pick any breathing method. It doesn't matter which one you choose. Eventually, you will develop more control over your mind.

"I would like to introduce you to another aspect of breath awareness called 'abdominal breathing.' You may have heard it referred to as 'belly breathing.' This is breathing fully into your abdomen instead of just into your chest. Let me explain this a bit.

"When your diaphragm moves to let you inhale, it pushes downward on the organs in your stomach cavity. This draws the air into your lungs. The abdomen should expand as you inhale. However, because many people carry tension in the stomach area, the abdominal muscles limit the amount of air that can be taken in during one inhalation by allowing only the upper portion of the lungs to expand.

"Watch and I'll show you what I mean. Try it with me. Put your two hands, one over the other, on top of your stomach. We'll do chest breathing first. Breathe in and let your shoulders lift as you take a deep breath. Notice how your chest expands but your hands hardly move. When this happens, your lungs are not filling completely.

"Now let's see what abdominal breathing is like. As you inhale, consciously push your stomach out. You should feel your hands move. This tells you that your lungs are getting more room to expand.

"Next, as you exhale, sigh deeply. Sighing is the body's natural way to let go of stress and tension, as well as to thoroughly exhale in order to inhale a full breath the next time."

Jim commented, "Our company had a speaker on stress management who emphasized the same thing. I realize I get tense at work when a major project is due. Most of the time, I forget to do any of the breathing techniques I learned, but when I remember, they are very helpful."

Lisa said she played the flute as a child and had learned to do abdominal breathing then. She needed to take in large amounts of air to play her flute passages without a break.

"During this next week, practice these breathing exercises at home," I told the class. "Pick one method you like the best and use it for a few minutes. It will help you clear your mind.

"Then try meditating for a few minutes with your thought-free mind. The Chinese call this a state of 'no mind.' If you find yourself thinking about something once again, re-start the breathing exercise.

"Remember, this doesn't have to take a lot of time. If you do it for a few minutes, a couple of times a day, you will feel the benefits. It will have a calming influence on you, as well as provide you with a good basis for learning deeper forms of meditation. Gradually, increase the time you spend with it.

"Earlier, I summarized all the levels of consciousness that exist within a human being. At this time, I'd like to look more closely at the components of your personal self. You have probably heard of the terms 'ego' and 'psyche.' These are words that refer to the personal self."

THE BODY MIND

"The first level of consciousness includes your physical body, as well as your body mind. As we discussed earlier, the body mind is the part of you that automatically monitors your breathing, digestion, heart rate, and other functions, to keep your body running smoothly.

"The body mind operates through your physical senses to receive information about your environment. It is tuned into the physical world as well as the non-physical world, such as another person's emotions. It is on the alert to protect you through reflex and avoidance.

"Your body mind tells you that something isn't right through your 'gut feelings.' This alerts your thinking mind to take notice and determine what is wrong. It doesn't think or use judgment on its own.

"The body mind works at a level that is separate from your conscious mind. You are aware, or conscious, of what you think and how you feel. You are also aware of your body's movements.

"Your body mind, however, functions beyond your conscious awareness. You do not have to tell your heart to beat or your lungs to breathe. They function automatically. The body mind can be said to exist at the level of your *un*-conscious. Sometimes it is called your sub-conscious.

"There are many examples of how the body mind works. If your skin gets scraped or cut, the body mind sends white blood cells to the area to prevent infection. If you need sleep, it makes you aware of your weariness so you will go to bed. When you sleep, it lets your muscles relax so your body can revitalize, grow, and repair tissue. The body mind is also the source of your instincts, such as the instinct to survive.

"The body mind has another unique characteristic, which is its ability to be easily programmed. It takes in information like a sponge. It relies on beliefs and decisions you make. Positive affirmations such as 'I can do this' influence the body mind, as do negative self-statements. They are all stored in the body mind and can continue to influence you.

"Your body mind, along with every cell in your physical body, can be said to have its own sense of instinct and limited intelligence. This is what directs your reflexes so they automatically do what is best for your body.

"It also has the ability to remember. You have probably heard references to 'cellular memory' or 'muscle memory.' This refers to the memory of things you have learned to do in the past with your physical body, such as riding a bicycle. You never really forget how to do them. All of this is accumulated in the body mind."

Lisa raised a question. "When I was young, I was bitten by a dog. I have never really gotten over it. Is that a function of the body mind?"

"Yes, it is," I said. "This is an example of the body mind's memory abilities. It will remember fear resulting from a traumatic experience. If you have been attacked by a dog, the next time you are around another dog, you will have an automatic reaction to be on guard or fearful. It is all part of the protective instinct of the body mind.

"You are particularly sensitive to dogs soon after your experience of being bitten. If a dog walked up to you, your body mind would signal your muscles to tense up, in case you had to fight it off. Your stomach would knot up with fear. You would have other stress reactions, such as an increase in your breathing and heart rate. These all make it possible for you to run away, if necessary.

"If you continued to be around dogs without suffering another attack, the body mind would relax its caution. It would be re-programmed to be calmer, instead of readying you to fight or flee. But the body mind may never let you totally forget about the incident, however. There may always be a sense of caution or guardedness. This is why you say that you haven't really recovered from your experience. It is retained in the 'memory' of your body mind."

"My brother fought in the Vietnam War and saw a counselor because of it," Jane commented. "His condition was called 'post-traumatic stress syndrome.' This kind of thing sounds like something related to the body mind."

"It certainly is," I said. "That is another example of the way the body mind works. It can be programmed to be on alert during an extended period of trauma, such as a war or a natural disaster. The body mind develops a state of readiness as a means of protection.

"However, this can continue long after the ordeal is over. It remains apprehensive that the trauma is going to happen again. You might develop symptoms such as finding it difficult to fall or stay asleep. You may also have an exaggerated startle response. All these reactions occur because of the effect of body mind programming.

"The body mind is influenced not only by trauma, but also by things that happen in the normal course of your life. It can be conditioned to tense or relax as you go about your day. For example, during a coffee break at work, you can take a rest from what you are doing, get something to eat, and enjoy yourself. You have a pleasurable association with it. Just looking forward to your break can cause you to feel relaxed.

"You can also develop unpleasant associations. If you dislike your job or get anxious about school, you can develop what is referred to as 'Sunday night blues.' This results from dreading the Monday morning start of something that is unpleasant for you. If you stop working or attending school, the 'Sunday night blues' will go away, but it might take awhile.

"Negative experiences that are not traumatic and happen only once or occasionally are unlikely to exert any lasting effect on the body mind. You feel your feelings, and then they go away. You don't think much about them again. For example, if you attend a crowded function that is unpleasant for you, you forget about the discomfort once you have returned home. Only when something unpleasant happens over and over does it cause a conditioned effect on the body mind.

"Everyday habits you do without thinking, such as washing your hands or doing the dishes, are guided by the body mind. Because you have mastered these skills, you don't have to concentrate to do them successfully. Your mind can wander or you can carry on a conversation at the same time. The memory of what you have learned is stored in the body mind.

"Another example of how this type of memory works is when you are driving your car and your mind is preoccupied on a stressful event happening in your life. Because you aren't paying attention to your driving, you may find yourself on your well-traveled route to work or home, rather than the destination you originally set out for."

"I can't tell you the number of times this has happened to me," Jane said emphatically. "I have wondered if something was wrong with my mind. It's nice to know why it happens."

"What about reflexes to avoid pain?" Lisa asked. "It seems to me they would be a part of the body mind, too. For instance, when I am cooking, if I didn't have the desire to avoid pain, I might be less careful with my knives or the hot stove."

"I know what you mean," Don chimed in. "Doing construction work can be hard on your body, too. It would be easy to pull muscles or even break bones if the risk of pain weren't present to deter you from overstraining yourself."

"You're right. This is an important function of the body mind," I said.

"Are addictions caused by programming of the body mind?" asked Lisa.

"Yes, to a significant degree," I responded. "For example, in alcoholism, counselors refer to the recurring desire to have a drink as the 'monkey on your back.' The 'monkey' is constantly whispering thoughts that not only suggest drinking, but also influence your mind to rationalize it."

Jane volunteered, "I can feel a strong urge to have chocolate if I have been in the routine of eating it every day. The reminder seems constant until I break the habit. Then it goes away, but it can take several days. I have to use a lot of will power to do it."

Jim asked, "Are emotional reactions a part of the body mind?"

"No, not technically," I said. "Emotions occur in the emotional body, but they are closely related to the body mind. The body mind triggers an emotional response along with its physical reaction. For example, if the body mind is calm, allowing your body to function smoothly, it contributes to a feeling of relaxation and well-being.

"On the other hand, if the body mind is on guard or stressed, the muscles and organs in your body are tense, as well. There is an accompanying feeling of uneasiness or apprehension. If the degree of disturbance in the body mind is very strong, severe anxiety or depression may result."

"That must be why I feel so uptight around my ex-husband," Jane commented. "I tense up, expecting us to get into a fight."

"Yes, that can happen," I said. "Feeling uneasy is an example of an emotional response triggered by tension in the body mind. As you can see on the chart of the personal self, the emotional body is the plane of consciousness next to the physical body. That is why reactions on these two planes are so interrelated."

THE EMOTIONAL BODY

"This brings us to a discussion of the next component of the personal self — the emotional body. As you already know, it is the vehicle for experiencing emotion.

"First of all, let me briefly define what an emotion is. An emotion is a discharge of energy in the emotional field. It results from reactions you have to situations that come up in life.

"Each emotion has its own level of energy and rate of vibration. You know from experience the energy from happiness is quite different from the energy of anger or depression. Happiness has a higher rate of vibration."

Al asked, "Is the emotional body also called the astral body or the aura?"

"Yes, it is," I said. "The word 'astral' refers to the stars. In the same way that you and I see the stars shine, those who have clairvoyant sight can see bright colors emitted by the emotional body. The astral body is primarily within your physical body, but it also extends several inches to a few feet beyond the surface of your skin.

"The emotional body has also been called the aura. An aura consists not only of a person's emotional body, however, but also of his or her mental and intuitional bodies. In addition, it is made up of excess vitality, or what is called 'prana,' emanating off the surface of an individual's skin. You can feel your body's energy, as well as its heat, if you hold your hand close to your skin.

"Try it on yourself. Hold your palm about a half an inch away from your arm or the palm of your other hand. Do you feel the energy?"

As the class experimented, Don grimaced. "I'm not sure I'm feeling anything," he said. "I feel heat, but I don't think I feel any other kind of energy."

"That's fine," I said. "It may be hard to sense at first. Try this. Hold the palms of your hands facing each other and about five inches apart. Keep your hands in this position and move them back and forth a bit. If it helps, close your eyes. Do you feel a sense of pressure or a springiness between your hands?"

"I can feel it," said Jim. "I definitely sense something between my hands. If I move one hand away and direct it to the center of the room, it feels quite different than when I hold it facing my other hand. The energy is subtle, but it is there."

"I am amazed at how much I can feel," remarked Jane. "It is as if my whole hand is one huge Geiger counter registering a reading throughout the entire surface. It is very strong."

"You people must be more sensitive than I," frowned Don.

"If you can't discern it, experiment a bit and see what you discover," I urged. "Take a little more time and play with it for a while. There is no 'right' way to go about it.

"Here's another technique. Try moving your palms close together and then opening them so they are about twelve inches apart. Slowly bring them close together again. Pay attention to what you feel. You may experience a tingling or a sense of pulsing in your hands. Each of you will perceive it in your own way."

After experimenting for a few minutes, Don said, "I didn't think I would feel anything, but after I moved my hands back and forth for awhile, I could sense something like a cloud between my hands. It was as if I was forming it when I moved my hands closer together. Then I wondered if I felt it because I was waving my hands. So I stopped them altogether and just noticed what it was like. It seemed to still be there, but only as heat. I'm not sure about any of this, though. Part of me is still skeptical."

"That's okay," I said. "It isn't necessary to feel anything in particular. This exercise is intended to introduce you to the subtle energy fields of the human body. What did others of you feel?"

Class members reported sensations ranging from a prickly feeling to a sense of coldness. All agreed they could feel some manifestation of the energetic field.

"Does the energy coming off the body feel different when a person goes through various emotional states?" asked Lisa.

"Yes," I said. "It changes when you are feel different emotions, as well as when you feel healthy or sick. It is all very subtle, though."

"I bet it is really hot when someone feels anger!" exclaimed Don.

"I agree," commented Lisa. "That reminds me of the expression 'He saw red.' Does that refer to the color of a person's face when he is mad, or does the color of the aura also turn red with anger?"

"A person's face can become red with anger," I said, "but the expression refers to the color of the emotional body. To someone who is clairvoyant, the color of anger is red.

"Each emotion has its own color. They range from dark and muddy colors that correspond to negative emotions to bright pastels. For example, brown is the color of selfishness and gray is depression. Contrasted to this is pink, which is the color of love and affection, and sky blue, which is the color of religious devotion."

"I have heard the expression 'green with envy.' This, too, must be a color of the aura, right?" Jane inquired.

"You're right," I said. "The color of envy is brownish-green.

"When your emotional body is quiet, its colors are from the emotions you have most of the time. If a sudden, strong feeling comes over you, such as devotion, the color blue will appear throughout your emotional body with the normal colors modifying the blue or appearing faintly through it. As the feeling dies away, so does the blue color. Yet the portion of blue normally in the astral body increases. This demonstrates how feeling a certain way will increase that quality in your nature."

Jane asked if I saw auras.

"No, I am not able to see auras," I answered. "What I have described to you is what I have learned from people who do. One reason I am sharing this with you is to show the relevance of expressions that associate colors with emotions."

"How does the emotional body change when you experience different emotions?" asked Al.

"When you are calm, you may be experiencing only a few different feelings in your emotional body," I said. "Each one has its own rate of vibration. If you have a strong emotion come over you, either positive or negative, your entire emotional body will vibrate to the level of that feeling. For example, if you remember someone who was kind to you, your emotional body will vibrate with love and appreciation.

"On the other hand, if you are stressed about something, you are likely to be experiencing quite a mixture of feelings. You may have twenty-five or more emotions all at once. This creates a sense of confusion and the need to 'sort out your feelings.' "

Jim was thinking about Anne when he asked, "What happens when you worry?"

"Worries cause areas of disturbance in your emotional body," I said. "They also drain your vitality. This is why spiritual teachers emphasize that you should try to be calm and serene as much as possible in your life. They teach that worry is useless because it doesn't do anything productive to solve your problems. It only makes you less able to face them. It is like the expression 'Don't cross the bridge before you come to it.' The best thing to do with worry is to try to reason out your problems and find solutions with the help of your higher mind."

"What is the effect of anger?" asked Don.

"When a person experiences any emotion, its energy is sent outward into the emotional field," I said. "If it is a strong, negative emotion, the vibrations are intense and can be sensed even at the physical level. This is described in the expression 'He makes my skin crawl.'

"If anger is expressed directly at someone, the effect is great. A saying describing this is 'He really dropped a bomb on me.'

"If two people are arguing, others nearby will be affected through the emotional field. Even if they cannot hear the argument, they can sense tension in the atmosphere. They will experience the sensation as unpleasant or uncomfortable.

"When children hear their parents argue, they not only are affected by the sounds of the argument, but they also receive the force of the strong emotions. Because of their young age, they are naturally more sensitive. They are also emotionally dependent upon their parents and thereby more connected to them. Babies may start crying when they hear arguments. Children affected by parental disagreements are said to be caught in 'emotional crossfire.' "

"When my parents argued, everyone in the family seemed to become argumentative," Jane reflected. "How does that happen?"

"People are swayed by the feelings of others. When a person feels an emotion, its energy is expressed in the emotional field. From there, it acts on other people's emotional bodies and stimulates them to feel or react in a similar way.

"If several people are experiencing the same emotional state, the effect on each individual is magnified. If this is at a church service, devotional feelings provide strength and support to all the members of the church. If this occurs in an angry crowd, the strength of the emotions promotes instability and a tendency toward violence.

"One characteristic of the emotional body is its fluidity. It moves easily from one emotion to another. Feelings arise and then dissipate. The expression 'This too shall pass' refers to the changing nature of an emotion.

"The emotional body is always fluctuating unless you hold on to a feeling by thinking about it over and over again in your mind. If you do this, your thoughts add energy to the emotion, making it stronger and more likely to come up again. You will recall we discussed how worry does this.

"The purpose of the emotional body is to feel your changing moods and dispositions. It responds to people you meet and events you participate in. It moves easily from feeling to feeling.

"One moment it may feel bored. Another moment it may feel angry as you remember an injustice. In yet another moment, it may feel excited as you look forward to something enjoyable. The emotional body does not act from reason, because it is independent of the mind. It just feels. That is its job.

"Let's move on to the next level of consciousness in the personal self. That is the mental body, which is the vehicle for the mind. This is how it functions."

THE MENTAL BODY

"As I have said, the mental body receives information from your body and your emotions, as well as from your environment. It interprets that information so you can understand it. It then puts it all together so you can solve problems, set goals, and plan strategies. This is how it directs your actions.

"Let me give you an example. Suppose you are at home. All of a sudden, you hear a loud rumble and your home begins to shake. Your body mind is alerted and your muscles tense up to be ready to react and move quickly. Your emotions express fear and alarm. Your mental body, or your mind, takes in all the information from your body, as well as from your immediate environment. It puts it together and determines an earthquake is occurring. It then decides where you should go to be safe.

"Your mind works closely with your body mind and your emotions. Because of this, it can be stimulated to be guarded and cautious. We discussed how the body mind sets off your protective instincts. This is what causes you to get defensive.

"If you put that together with your mind, with its natural inclination to be coherent and consistent, stubbornness can develop. Your mind will want you to maintain your position on an issue, even though change may be a better option. It will defend your opinions and prejudices. It will prefer to stick with one point of view rather than seem to waver. This is what influences you to rationalize yourself.

"When one of your opinions is challenged, your mind may try to ward off the sense of being threatened by becoming arrogant or egotistical. It doesn't want to be wrong. It can come across with a strong sense of pride."

"This must be what happens when I can't back down in an argument," Don admitted.

"I know what you mean, Don," Jim said. "For me, I fear losing face. Sometimes, I don't want to say I am wrong. Only after thinking something through I can see the light."

"Good insights!" I said. "You can see the mental body has its limitations. Your ability to reason and see where you make your mistakes comes from your higher mind. We'll be discussing that in awhile.

"In addition to understanding the mental body, I'd like to explain what a thought-form is. It is the natural result of the functioning of your mind.

"Whenever you think of anything, electrical energy moves along the neurons in your brain. This energy then emanates outward from your head. It continues in this fashion as long as you are engrossed in the same thought. This is what makes up a thought-form. It is a bundle of electrical energy created whenever you think, imagine, or daydream about something.

"When you are thinking one particular thought, the energy produced vibrates at its own unique rate. Each time you change your thought, you create a new thought-form which will have its own sense of structure and rate of vibration based on its content.

"After a thought-form is created and you stop thinking about the subject, the energy of the thought-form begins to dissipate. If your thought was weak and vague, the thought-form breaks up quickly. If your thought was clear and strong, the thought-form is more distinct and definite. It lasts longer before disintegrating.

"If several people think the same kind of thoughts, the energy in their thought-forms will harmonize because they have the same vibrational rate. If people continue to think alike, the group thought-form will enlarge and intensify. It will arouse similar thoughts in the mental bodies of others nearby, the same way the emotions of a group influence others to share the same emotion.

"A group of people can cause others to think the same way. It is relatively easy to be swayed to accept an idea others have created. More difficult is the process of considering various aspects of something to decide exactly what you think about it.

"It is even easier to be influenced by a group if emotion is connected to the thinking. This strengthens the thought-form. You join the line of thought as if you were being swept up in a river's strong current.

"This is how peer pressure works. The pressure comes from several people thinking a certain way. They don't even have to pressure you to join them. Their thoughts persuade you to go along with what they think or feel about something.

"Peer pressure can sway you to do or think things you normally wouldn't. Its influence, although subtle, can be very compelling. It takes strength of will and clarity of your own thought to go against it.

"The kind of thoughts you are in the habit of thinking will tend to reproduce themselves again and again in your mind. This is caused by many things, but largely results from the energy of your own thought-forms. They linger around you and contribute to habitual thinking patterns.

"For example, if you worry about something, you create a thought-form about it. The thought-form stimulates the idea to reappear in your mind. The more you think about it, the more energy you add to it, making it more likely to come up again. It is a circular process. It can be broken at the end of the day by going to sleep. Then the energy in the thought-form dissipates.

"The expression 'You will feel better in the morning' reflects this. But if you awaken and start thinking about the previous day's worries, you revitalize the thought-forms with new energy. Then they are ready to trouble you again.

"The influence of thought is great. Proverbs 23:7 in the Bible expresses it, 'As a man thinketh, so goes he.' "

Al commented, "That reminds me of the expression 'You walk your thoughts.' "

"Yes, that says the same thing," I said. "Since the power your thinking patterns have over you is strong, you should choose your thoughts carefully. Then you will have some control over what you are likely to think about in the future.

"We will discuss specific things you can do to monitor and change this in the fourth class."

"This makes me think about what it feels like inside a church," Al reflected. "Each has its own unique atmosphere. Usually what I sense is a devotional and peaceful feeling. Is this caused by thought-forms?"

"Yes, they contribute to it," I said. "The architecture of the church and the symbolism of the altar also suggest certain kinds of reactions, but the energy from the thought-forms of the people who have worshipped there can be perceived.

"The mental plane has another interesting characteristic that I'm sure you are all aware of — the absence of time. Let me explain what this means.

"Thoughts take place immediately on the mental plane because time and space are not present to impede your mind's activity. The minute you think of something, it is there. An example of this is cooking dinner. It takes no time at all to think of preparing a meal. In one instant, it is done. But it takes a lot longer to actually do it."

"What happens when you think of a particular person?" asked Al. "Does the energy of your thought affect them in any way?"

"Let me explain what I have been taught about this," I said. "If you think of someone in a particular way, the thought-form 'travels' instantly through the mental plane to the person and blends with his mental body. If he is thinking of nothing specific, it will arouse similar vibrations in him. It tends to create the same kind of thought in his mental body. If his mind is thinking of something similar to your thought-form, his thought will be strengthened. If his mind is already occupied with something else, the thought-form will influence him when his mind is free. This accounts for one of the reasons why thoughts suddenly come up in your mind.

"If you send love to someone, for example, the force of your love is transferred through the thought-form. The person will be aroused with the feeling of affection and his or her power of loving will increase slightly. Sending love to someone also strengthens the power of affection in you.

"The same happens with other feelings, such as anger. They are 'sent' to people you think of. Spiritual teachers emphasize the importance of monitoring your thoughts so you don't convey negative feelings to others. Thoughts are transmitted like words and travel everywhere."

Jim said, "I am reminded of the saying I heard as a child, 'If you can't say anything nice, don't say anything at all.' It sounds like you're saying that people need to watch what they think, too. The expression should be 'If you can't think anything nice, don't think anything at all.' "

"That is so true," I agreed.

"This must be the reason a prayer circle can help people who are injured or ill," noted Al. "I have heard about a group of people praying for someone and being able to help improve their health faster and with fewer complications than if he or she didn't receive any prayers at all."

"You're right, Al," I said. "Research has led to this conclusion."

"What about intuition? How does that come about?" asked Jim.

THE HIGHER MIND

"Intuition is centered in your higher mental body," I said. "You may recall that within the mental body there is your lower mind, which deals with your ordinary, everyday thoughts, as well as your higher mind, which links you to your intuition and higher reasoning powers.

"Your everyday mind processes the thoughts you generate as you go about your day-to-day activities. It focuses on concrete things you do and say. It is not able to perceive the subtleties your higher mind can understand. It is obtuse and does not readily discern things that are not apparent to the eye.

"For example, it decides you are separate from others. All it notices is where one body ends and another starts. It doesn't understand any of the connections you have with others, such as the feeling of unity in a family. It cannot see the whole picture. It only looks at the individual components.

"This is due to the nature of your mind. It discriminates between things. It divides and opposes. It is the higher mind that unites and harmonizes. It sees the whole with the parts, and the part as directly connected to the whole.

"Take the example of the sense of separation between people. It is only natural for your everyday mind to recognize differences. It picks up on the way people look and talk, as well as their customs and habits. You notice the unfamiliar. You may even feel threatened because of the protective instinct of your body mind.

"The higher mind sees similarities as well as differences. It generates the spirit of synthesis. It recognizes we are one humanity. Its influence allows you to get along with people who are different from you or with members of your family you may not always agree with.

"This happens because the higher mind is your connection to the field of Unity. It comes from love, which is the manifestation of Unity. Love brings people together and creates the spirit of oneness.

"The quality of discrimination inherent in your everyday mind is essential for your development. It has a special purpose. It is necessary in the process of learning to judge what is right and wrong.

"Take the example of helping someone who has fallen down. Your everyday mind knows the difference between walking away or bending down to help. Your higher mind understands why you do what is 'right.' Again, this comes from the influence of the field of Unity. You treat the other person as you would want to be treated.

"Another way this shows up is your ability to understand someone by 'putting yourself into his shoes.' It enables you to actually unify with the person you are thinking about or interacting with. Your higher mind gives you *in*-sight, or the ability to see into something. Then you truly know why the other person acts and feels the way he does. This includes yourself. Your higher mind is the part of you that makes self-analysis possible.

"Another important aspect of your higher mind is its ability to understand the changeable nature of your everyday mind. You can decide you dislike something one day and then change your mind to like it the next. For example, when you first tried coffee, it may have tasted bitter to you. But with repeated attempts at drinking it, you learned to like it. It becomes acceptable to you. It is your higher mind that understands this inconsistency.

"The lower mind makes an assessment of what you think about things. It determines if you are an advocate for something or in opposition to it. It colors your world in its own way. However, your higher mind doesn't let you get stuck in limited ways of thinking. It keeps your mind open.

"For example, when you first meet someone, you feel separate from him. If you fall in love, he becomes your own Self, as you become 'one' with him. If you quarrel, your mind decides he is your enemy.

"The higher mind knows the true nature of all this. It understands the influence of your emotional defenses which cause you to think someone is against you. The higher mind provides the wisdom that enables you to see the truth."

"I wish I had known about this when I went through my divorce," Jane said. "Now I realize my ex-husband was acting the way he did because of his hurt feelings. At the time, I felt overwhelmed. I couldn't understand what was going on."

"Yes, it is hard to hear your intuition when you are going through a difficult time," I said. "We will learn more about that later.

"Let us close for now. Be sure to practice your breathing techniques and meditation!"

The Purpose of Life

"At one time or another, each of you probably has wondered about the meaning of your existence. You may have asked yourself, 'Who am I?' 'Why am I here?' 'What is the reason for living?' These are tough questions. Let me address the first question briefly, since we discussed it in the first class.

" 'Who am I?'

"You are a spirit within a body. The spiritual part of you is your spiritual Self. The means of expressing your spiritual Self on the physical plane is through your personal self. The personal self is your body, along with your body mind, your emotions, and your thinking mind.

" 'Why am I here?'

"This question is harder to answer. Let me give you some background before we explore it further.

"You are alive because the spiritual essence within you is naturally attracted to life in material form. It yearns to exist on the physical plane where it can live in the world of form and structure. But in order to do this, it must have a body to live in. This is your personal self. It needs your body and mind to exist in the world.

"This is part of a universal cycle where spirit comes to live in physical form and then returns to unify with the Universal Spirit. This process has been going on since 'the beginning of time.' It will never end. It mirrors the continual change inherent in all aspects of life.

"You know things always change in the physical world. You see it in the change of seasons and in physical growth and development. Nothing stays the same. There is perpetual movement, either from growth and expansion or from decline and death.

"The same is true on the spiritual plane. Change happens naturally and continually. Spiritual essence seeks expression in physical reality, then yearns to merge back into spiritual unity."

THE EVOLUTION OF SPIRIT INTO MATTER

"Why does spirit want to become physical?" Lisa asked. "Living in the world means dealing with pain and problems. Why doesn't it remain where everything is peaceful and wonderful?"

"I know what you mean," I concurred. "It seems spirit would want to avoid the suffering that happens in earthly life. Once, when I was engaged in a philosophical discussion about this topic, a person said heaven didn't sound all that great to her. She said it may be beautiful and serene, but it would also be boring. It would be too monotonous. She wanted to be able to sing and laugh — and you need a body to do this."

The group laughed and made a couple of comments about how funny it was to think about heaven being boring. A few people said the topic was so new to them they didn't know what to think.

"By the way, you develop spiritually when you ponder these things," I said. "The famous French chemist and bacteriologist, Louis Pasteur, said, 'To know how to wonder and question is the first step of the mind toward discovery.' Every time you think about the deeper aspects of life, you open yourself up, in small degrees, to the intuitional field. It widens your connection to it.

"Manifesting on the physical plane allows your spiritual essence to be known. It longs to feel its existence in a more complete way. Life in a physical body provides a definiteness and a precision that does not exist on any other plane. It is tangible. The vibrations of the higher planes are too rapid to be truly felt, just as ultraviolet rays are too rapid to be seen with the physical eye.

"At the spiritual level, there is no thinking, feeling, or moving, because these are done with a mind and a body. Spirit simply *is*. By being in the body, spiritual essence can experience physical vibrations that make it feel alive.

"This is beautifully stated in the traditional Islamic saying, 'I was a hidden treasure and I longed to be known. So I created you.'

"Kahlil Gibran, in *The Prophet*, also expresses it: 'Your children are not your children. They are the sons and daughters of Life's longing for itself.'

"When spirit manifests in physical form, it undergoes a long process of evolution before it is instilled in a human body. Spiritual essence then takes form as consciousness.

"At the beginning, the consciousness is undeveloped and barely aware of its existence. It operates out of a survival instinct. Because it is weak and uncertain, it needs the help of a strong sense of self-preservation until it becomes firmly established.

"This is seen in a human being in the first part of its development. It shows up in self-centeredness and selfishness. This may seem like a hindrance rather than a helpful quality, but it is an important step in an individual's progress. Without it, the developing human would be in danger of annihilation.

"Self-centeredness insures survival. It is only natural for you to think about 'me, my, and mine.' This is the spiritual essence building a strong center of individuality. The selfishness acts as protection, like a cocoon protecting a developing butterfly or moth. Eventually, the butterfly matures and breaks through the cocoon to live in the world.

"Likewise, your consciousness eventually breaks through the protective cocoon of selfishness. You are free from operating only from a position of self-interest. You can express unselfishness. However, the inclination to give to others comes only after a strong sense of self has been formed.

"The protective cocoon in you is your personal self. This is your body, along with the body mind, the emotional body, and the lower mental body. These all act to insure your survival. They are essential in order for your spiritual essence to exist on the physical plane.

"The personal self is like the cocoon that allows a larva to transform into a butterfly. The cocoon of your instinctive, personal self allows your consciousness to develop and eventually live as an expression of your spiritual Self.

"Just like the butterfly has to struggle to break out of its cocoon, your developing consciousness has to persist at overcoming its self-centeredness. Like a cocoon, the protective selfishness is strong. It resists efforts to be selfless and giving. It has worked a long time with you and only you as its prime concern.

"You can see this in yourself if you feel disinclined to help someone in trouble. The part of you that doesn't want to be bothered is your cocoon. It warns you not to be late for where you're going and says someone else can give assistance. But the spiritual part of you that feels love and compassion is your butterfly. It responds when someone is in need.

"Another example of how your cocoon operates is when you preserve your place in line at an entrance to an amusement park or a concession stand. The instinctive personal self will be protective and prevent others from crowding. It watches out for your needs. If you see someone who is handicapped come up, however, your consciousness is guided by your spiritual Self as you allow him or her to join the line in front of you."

"It sounds like the personal self must be at the root of all problems in life," Lisa commented. "If it makes you self-centered, then it can only be a hindrance, rather than a help."

"It may seem that way," I said, "but the personal self serves a necessary purpose. Problems arise when your consciousness gets wrapped up in that point of view and prevents you from using your intelligence and wisdom. Let me explain this more fully.

"The personal self has an important job to do. Through your body and body mind, it tells you how to take care of yourself. It uses your emotional body to let you know how you feel and when you are comfortable and happy. Through your mental body, it organizes your life, makes plans, and finds ways to carry them out. These aspects allow you to function. However, your consciousness doesn't have to operate only from the standpoint of your personal self. You have the ability to think and reason out how you want to interact in the world.

"As I have said, your intelligence is the intermediary between your instinctive, personal self and your spiritual Self. With your intelligence, you monitor the input from the urges of your personal self and *decide* how you want to feel or think.

"So the purpose of life is to develop your consciousness in order to *use* the personal self to live, but to be *guided* by your spiritual Self.

"This is essentially the answer to the third question we asked at the beginning of the class, 'What is the purpose for living?'

"The purpose of your existence is to discover your own divine spiritual nature and learn to live in a way that expresses that divinity. You are here to use your personal self *to express the qualities of your spiritual Self.*

"Understanding this can be difficult. Because of its complexity, stories, myths, and metaphors have traditionally been used to explain the process. One of these is the metaphor of the seed placed in the soil. This is symbolic of the spiritual Self concealed within the physical body and personality. At first, you are living in darkness because the spiritual Self, protected by the survival instinct, is hidden under selfishness. You are unable to express the qualities of unselfishness. The same is true with a seed. Before it can grow, it must spend time beneath the earth in darkness.

"A tree is latent in the seed, just like the flowering of the spiritual Self is latent within each person. As the shell of the seed is broken, the tree sprouts. Its blossoms have a scent, which is said to be the breath of God. The same thing happens to you. As the shell of selfishness in your personal self opens up, your spiritual Self blooms and allows you to be an expression of its love."

Al commented, "This sounds like the Greek myth of Persephone, who has to descend into the underworld every winter to be the bride of Hades. When she returns to her mother, Demeter, spring returns to the world."

"Yes, you're right," I said. "Persephone represents the seed as it germinates beneath the soil. It is also a metaphor for the life force in the world. When Persephone is in the underworld, it symbolizes your spiritual Self enclosed in the darkness of your self-centeredness. Hades, the ruler of the underworld, represents desire, which is the result of your selfishness and the cause of most of your problems.

"Another traditional story is the description of Adam and Eve in the Garden of Eden. In the Garden of Eden, everything is perfect. It is as wondrous as heaven. Eve offers Adam an apple from the Tree of Knowledge. He eats it, and commits a 'sin.' This is a metaphor for the spiritual Self being hampered in its expression by the personal self. As Adam masters his desires, he gains knowledge and is able to express his spiritual Self.

"Another myth is the story in the Gospel of St. Thomas. This gospel, written on papyrus, was found in 1945 in a cave in Egypt. It was part of a discovery of other early Christian texts known as the Gnostic Gospels, such as the Gospel of Philip.

"The Gospel of St. Thomas describes a man's arduous and lengthy search for a special pearl of high value. He runs into many obstacles and problems on his way. In this allegory, the pearl is symbolic of the spiritual Self within. The problems encountered during the search represent difficulties that need to be overcome due to the self-centeredness of the personal self.

"The same theme is expressed in the myths about a hero on a long journey. He must conquer dragons and demons as he goes about his travels. The evil monsters symbolize selfish tendencies and other emotional difficulties. The 'journey' is the process of the hero becoming one with his spiritual Self.

"A small book written by Alcyone, or Krishnamurti, entitled *At the Feet of the Master*, contains some words of wisdom. It says that, as you develop and express the qualities of your spiritual Self, you become 'a pen in the hand of God, through which His thought may flow and find for itself an expression down here, which without a pen it could not have.'[1] At first, you, as the pen, don't know what you are writing. As your consciousness develops and you transcend the limited view of your personal self, you can actively manifest your divine nature."

Al commented, "As I ponder what you are saying, it sounds like the only thing I can do with my life is to live it. You say the personal self is necessary in order to live and problems are bound to come up. Since this is the only way I can learn, it all must be part of the process."

"That is exactly right," I said. "You have stated it perfectly. Living is life's only purpose. You are discovering all the time. As you go about your life, by trial and error you learn what works and what doesn't. Even if you make no specific attempts to better yourself, a constant learning occurs nevertheless, which contributes to your evolution.

"Life is like a tapestry. The lengthwise threads of the tapestry come from and go on into infinity. The spiritual Self is the inspiration as you weave the crosswise threads. Each day is one thread. At first, you don't understand what you are doing with your life. You might try different things, in a sense, experimenting with different colored threads. The appearance of the tapestry may seem chaotic. But as you begin to realize why the patterns in the tapestry appear as they do, you learn to live in ways that are harmonious with your inner nature. Then the design of the tapestry becomes beautiful."

"What about free will?" asked Jane. "How does that enter into the scheme of things?"

FREE WILL

"Free will is a necessary part of life. I am sure you are aware of it within yourself. You are not a robot, acting under the control of some outside force. You make your own choices. Sometimes your emotions may seem to control you, but you have the power to choose what you do or say.

"In order for the human consciousness to develop, it must act on its own. If it were controlled by an outside force, it would not evolve. Consciousness grows and matures because of the choices you make as you go through your life. You become conscious of the consequences of your actions and learn which way is best.

"For example, if a husband uses his position of authority to dominate his wife and family through fear, he must see the error in his ways himself. It is possible that he may not want to change during his whole life. More often than not, however, he realizes he is doing something wrong, particularly if he has lost close relationships along the way. The tendency may be there for the man to justify and rationalize his point of view. It is easy to blame others. But this is merely the defensiveness of the instinctive self. The wise part of the man knows his responsibility in the matter.

"Losses are life's way to teach. One analogy I have heard about this is that the lessons learned by your consciousness through problems and setbacks are not obstacles, but stepping stones toward development.

"This is where therapy can be helpful. Therapy allows you to vent your pain and frustrations. As these feelings are expressed, there is a relaxation of your defensiveness. In looking at your past actions, you can see how you made your mistakes. You learn to understand why you act the way you do. This helps set the stage for you to use the personality as a tool for what you decide to do from the guidance of your spiritual Self."

Don asked, "But how are we supposed to act toward others? Are we supposed to like everyone the same? It doesn't seem possible. In my life, I enjoy being around some people and can't stand others!"

"Certainly you will like some people more than others," I responded. "There's nothing wrong with that. But the purpose of life is to live in harmony with all. This does not mean you must feel the same affection toward every individual. That's unrealistic. The goal is to feel a lack of hostility and a friendly attitude toward everyone."

"But what if there is someone you have a real problem with?" Jane inquired. "Suppose you have tried everything you can think of to get along, but nothing works."

"There are two things you can do in a situation like this," I answered. "First, when you say the words 'someone you have a problem with,' examine yourself to determine why he or she bothers you. Notice what feelings come up in yourself. Analyze your reactions that are triggered by the other person.

"Secondly, you should try to understand the people you are in a conflict with. See if you can figure out why they act the way they do. Talk to them about their lives. When you know more about their personal circumstances, you soften your defenses. You begin to see them more neutrally and with feelings of compassion. This can start the process of healing between you."

REINCARNATION

"At this time, I would like to introduce the concept of reincarnation. It is relevant to the discussion of the purpose of our existence. However, let me say I am presenting it to you as a theory. I do not expect you to believe it just because I am describing it to you. If you cannot accept it, merely listen with an open mind, consider its ramifications, and hear it as one possibility of many. Even if the rest of the class accepts it, you should believe it only if it is in accordance with your own intuition.

"If you are unsure of the validity of reincarnation, you can apply what I am saying about evolution to what someone would learn during his or her entire lifetime. Or you can generalize the concepts and apply them to the development of humanity as a whole.

"Reincarnation is the theory that says after the death of the physical body, your consciousness has the opportunity to come back to life on earth again in a new body. Because each lifetime is one incarnation, in consecutive lifetimes your consciousness *re*-incarnates into different bodies."

Lisa said, "I have never heard of the word 'incarnation.' Can you expand on that?"

"Sure," I said. "As you go about your daily life, you are living in a body of flesh and bones. It can be said you are incarnate, or embodied in a human form of muscles, fat, bones, and skin. Each lifetime, or incarnation, is only one of many your spiritual Self will have as it goes through its development. After each life and death, the process of the spiritual Self returning to live in a new body is reincarnation.

"Your consciousness evolves during each life existence. Because the process of development is so involved, there is no way you can learn everything in one lifetime. This is due to the nature of the physical plane. Evolution is slow because matter is dense. Your consciousness operating within your physical brain becomes aware and open to its spiritual nature only gradually. Because the physical body grows old and wears out, there isn't enough time for the consciousness to fully mature. It has to be done over many lifetimes.

"Reincarnation provides a process for this. In addition, it furnishes a new personality for you to use each time. Because the characteristics of each personality are unique, it allows the spiritual Self to perfect its expression by developing a different set of attributes each lifetime. It takes many personalities together to develop all the potential qualities of your spiritual Self.

"For example, one lifetime may provide circumstances for you to develop patience. Another may allow you to develop your thinking and reasoning powers. Yet another may help you develop your creativity. Altogether, they evolve a perfect vehicle of consciousness representing every aspect of your divine nature.

"You have all the qualities of your spiritual Self within you. Your personality is a unique mix of traits emphasizing a portion of those qualities. Each lifetime, new or different qualities are enhanced. It is like a kaleidoscope. Every turn of the kaleidoscope creates a new picture of dazzling colors and shapes. This symbolizes a new personality which brings out the light of the spiritual Self in its own unique way.

"Charles W. Leadbeater, in *A Textbook of Theosophy*, describes the development of the spiritual Self in the following metaphor. He says each life is like a day in school. The spiritual Self puts on a garment of flesh and goes to school in the physical world to learn certain lessons. The garment of flesh is the personal self.

"At the end of the 'school day,' the spiritual Self puts aside the garment of flesh and returns home for rest and refreshment. This is the heaven world. In the 'morning' of each new life, the spiritual Self takes up the lessons at the point where it left off the 'night' before.

"The spiritual Self may learn some lessons on the physical plane completely in one lifetime. Other lessons may require several lifetimes. At the end of its education, it merges, fully evolved, into the heaven world. No student fails. Each one goes on to the end. The length of time it takes is each individual's choice."[2]

Lisa asked, "I have heard it said that we, as human beings, originally started out our evolution as lower beings, maybe even plants. What do you think?"

"Teachers say the spiritual Self has already passed through the mineral, vegetable, and animal kingdoms before ending up in the human kingdom," I said. "They teach that this is the progression for the evolving life force. It is referred to as the transmigration of the soul.

"Jalaluddin Rumi, the Persian poet, wrote about this in the following poem:

> "A stone I died and rose again a plant;
> "A plant I died and rose an animal
> "I died an animal and was born a man.
> "Why should I fear? What have I lost by death?[3]

"In *Talks on the Path of Occultism*, Charles Leadbeater uses another metaphor to describe reincarnation. He says one lifetime on earth is like an actor in one stage performance. When the actor is finished with his performance, he goes home to live. This is what is referred to as his 'real' life.[4]

"Likewise, your day-to-day life on earth is your stage life. When you are not in your costume and makeup — your body and personality — you are living your 'real' life in your spiritual Self in what may be called 'heaven.' Just as the actor wishes to do well on stage, you wish to develop and do well in your temporary, physical life on earth.

"Each performance on stage is the same as one incarnation. The evolution of the spiritual Self spans many lifetimes. It is like the career of an actor, which covers many performances over the years.

"The poet William Wordsworth, in *Imitations of Immortality*, said of reincarnation:

> "Our birth is but a sleep and a forgetting:
> "The soul that rises with us, our life's Star,
>> "Hath had elsewhere its setting,
>>> "And comes from afar."

"Why can't we remember our past lives?" Lisa queried.

"Because the memories of one lifetime are stored in the physical brain," I explained. "When the body dies at the end of your life, the brain's memories also die. They do not carry over into the next incarnation.

"The same is true for all you have acquired in the form of 'book learning.' This is what you have been taught or read. It also is gone when your brain dies. What does carry over is the knowledge of things in the abstract that is preserved in your spiritual Self. What you have studied in a previous lifetime will be easily understood in succeeding incarnations because it will be 'remembered' intuitively.

"Plato wrote about this when he said, 'Knowledge easily acquired is that which the enduring Self had in an earlier life. It flows back easily.' "

Lisa asked, "Is this the reason some people are gifted with a special talent, such as Beethoven and his ability to compose music?"

"Yes," I answered. "It is said those who have natural abilities developed them in past lives. They are retained in the spiritual Self so that relearning something similar is easy."

"A friend of mine is very curious about her past lives," Jane mentioned. "I have never really cared about them. What do you think about it?"

"Curiosity about your past lives is understandable," I said. "However, not being able to remember them is a good thing. Think of all the problems you have in your current life. If you were to add to that the memories of your problems from past lives, you would feel tremendously burdened. There is enough to deal with in one life at a time. Nature has a way of making life easy to bear because of the way we 'start over' each lifetime."

"Is there information about reincarnation in the Bible?" asked Jim.

"Yes," I answered. "In fact, reincarnation was part of the early Christian teachings until the middle of the sixth century. At that time, Emperor Justinian of Rome declared the belief in reincarnation to be heretical and punishable by excommunication from the church. This was in 533 C.E.

"By the way, 'C.E.' stands for 'Common Era,' which is a more universal way of saying 'A.D.' or 'anno Domini,' which translates as 'in the year of our Lord.' This refers to Jesus Christ. Currently, scholars are using the abbreviations 'C.E.' and 'B.C.E.' for 'Common Era' and 'Before Common Era.' These expressions are more neutral becuase they don't refer to any one religious figure.

"Emperor Justinian had made himself the head of the church. He was in a powerful position as the agent of God to his subjects. He saw the belief in reincarnation as a threat to that position of authority. So he banned the belief."

"Why did he think that the belief in reincarnation threatened him?" Lisa inquired.

Al offered, "You have to think about the influence of the church back in those days. It was very powerful. The church had rules about most aspects of life. The teaching about reincarnation basically said that everyone had equal access to the heaven world through his or her normal evolution, and people didn't need the church as a mediator to intervene on their behalf. That's why the church's position of power and authority seemed threatened."

"Well stated," I said. "There is quite a lot of information available about the history of the early Christian church. My purpose in speaking about this is to make you aware that the concept of reincarnation is not found exclusively in the Eastern traditions of Hinduism and Buddhism. It is also in the Christian tradition.

"The Bible contains some references to reincarnation. John 9:2 says, 'And his disciples asked him, saying, "Master, who did sin, this man, or his parents, that he was born blind?" ' This questions whether the man's blindness was caused by his sin in a previous incarnation or was due to his parents' sin.

"Matthew 17:12–13 reads, ' "But I say unto you, that Elias is come already, and they knew him not, but have done unto him whatsoever they listed. Likewise shall also the Son of man suffer of them." Then the disciples understood that he spoke unto them of John the Baptist.' This verse refers to John the Baptist as being a reincarnation of Elias.

"Let's take a break for now. Then we'll start up again with another meditation."

THE PURPOSE OF MEDITATION

"Last week, I led you through some breathing exercises to introduce you to the fundamentals of meditation. Tonight, we will be taking a deeper look at meditation.

"If you recall, concentrating on your breath provides a focus so you won't get preoccupied with all the thoughts that normally crowd your mind. They are endless. By nature, your mind is constantly active.

"The persistent activity of the mind is referred to in the sacred book of Hinduism, the Bhagavad-Gita. It says, 'The mind is verily restless. . . . I deem it as hard to curb as the wind.'⁵ This is a perfect metaphor for the unstoppable mind. To reach a state of quiet and tranquillity, you must transcend the mind.

"The ultimate goal of meditation is to get in touch with the stillness at the core of your spiritual Self. However, this is far easier said than done. It takes practice. It must be worked on over time.

"In meditation, you suspend your thinking and feelings about your day-to-day life. You focus your mind on the peace within you. You tune out sounds from your environment.

"It is like reading a book and not responding to events happening around you. While meditating, your perception is focused on the quietness of your being. This focus is said to be one-pointed. Let me give you an example that will explain what this means.

"Did you ever have a 'stare-down' contest when you were young? This is a game where you stare into someone's eyes and try not to be the one who blinks first. If you blink, you lose. When you do this, you must pay careful attention to make sure you don't blink. You can say your mind is one-pointed. This means you are focusing on only one thing — to keep your eyes open.

"In the contest, the one-pointedness keeps your mind from wandering, which would cause your body to act normally and let your eyes blink. This is the same thing you do in meditation. You pay careful attention to the quietness within. You suspend thinking about day-to-day matters so your mind can become one-pointed and aware only of the silence of your basic essence. Then you are open to your true Self.

"One-pointed attention is referred to in the saying from Africa, 'The one who never stops talking becomes silent when walking through thorns.'⁶ When walking barefoot in Africa, in order to prevent getting stuck in the foot with a thorn, you must concentrate so you walk gently and carefully. Idle chatter distracts you from paying attention to how you are placing your feet. The same is true with meditation. You stop thinking idle and insignificant thoughts, which enables you to pay attention to your inner stillness."

"Should you concentrate your mind on anything?" asked Jane.

"Technically, meditation is not concentration," I said. "Concentrating your thoughts narrows your mind because you become engrossed in what you are focusing on. On the contrary, the purpose of meditation is to *widen* your mind. When you are meditating, it might seem like you are concentrating on the peacefulness within you. Actually, you are just maintaining the state of being disengaged from your thoughts. This lets you keep your mind open to your spiritual essence.

"Let us look at an example. If you concentrate on stopping your thoughts, you must make an effort to resist thinking. When you restrain yourself from thinking, you are using your everyday mind. You notice your success and failure in how long you have gone without an intrusive thought. There is a striving toward a goal.

"In meditation, you merely open yourself up. It is not about accomplishing anything. That would be like trying to have an experience that is different from what already exists. In meditation, you simply relax into it. You only have to be aware of awareness itself."

"Is breath awareness concentration?" Jane asked.

"In a way, it is," I said. "But you use it only to take you out of your routine thinking patterns to get some control over your mind. Being aware of your breath isn't the goal in itself. It is merely a means to an end.

"Let me see if I can help you understand what I mean when I ask you to focus on your awareness.

"Direct your gaze out this window. Don't look at anything in particular. Widen the focus of your eyes to see all the way to the edge of your peripheral vision. Absorb the peace and tranquillity of the trees and the sky. Take a deep breath and relax. Be aware that your thoughts are suspended. This leaves room for you to notice the stillness within."

After a pause, I asked, "Did this make sense? Were you able to let go and settle into your awareness?"

The class was quiet and a few people nodded. Lisa commented, "I think I know what you mean. Are you saying I should simply be aware of myself looking out the window?"

When I nodded, she said, "It seems so easy."

"Yes, that is all you have to do," I said. "It really is easy. The hard part is holding on to it."

"When I did what you asked," Al said, "it was as if the objects I saw out your window held no importance. I didn't focus on anything in particular. All I felt was peaceful. Is this what you are getting at?"

"Yes," I answered. "Normally, meditation is done with your eyes closed so you don't get caught up in watching things that will engage your mind. This time, I wanted to use the trees and the sky so you could be aware of the beauty of nature."

"It sounds like meditation can be used in a variety of ways. Is that so?" Jim asked.

"Yes," I said. "You can meditate to relax, or to aid your healing processes. You can meditate to send loving thoughts to another. But ultimately, meditation is for you to get in tune with your spiritual Self. As you do this, you become more and more familiar with it. You learn you can return to it whenever you want. Gradually, the awareness of its peace and serenity will start to pervade your entire nature."

Lisa said, "I have heard the expression of people becoming 'centered.' Is this similar to what you are talking about?"

"Yes," I answered. "It means becoming centered in your spiritual Self. When this happens, you are able to see the larger picture in life instead of being wrapped up in what is happening at the moment. You develop a sense of detachment and acceptance to what is going on. There is an inner strength you can tap into to help you cope with life's problems. Within the awareness you just experienced is where you will find that strength."

Don voiced some doubt. "How can feeling your awareness help you cope with a problem you have?"

"I can understand your question," I told him. "It may seem like quite a stretch to believe it could have an impact. Nevertheless, it works, because within the state of awareness, there is no thought or feeling, and thus no pain. There is just a quiet watching. It is the same as the expression of 'turning your problems over to God.'

"When you meditate, you detach yourself from your problems for a short time. That in itself is calming. In addition, when you are done meditating, even if it was for only a short time, the calm you acquired remains with you. Inevitably, your mind will get caught up once again in your everyday concerns. This is normal. But you can return to the state of being 'centered' any time you wish.

"If you have a problem with something, stepping back from it will allow you to see solutions more clearly. This comes from a sense of indifference. The more you do it, the easier it becomes. Believe me, it is better than worrying about something. Worry only causes you to worry more. This is due to the nature of your mind. It will tend to repeat what it was just doing."

"I have heard about people meditating on a problem," Al commented. "How does that work?"

"You can use meditation to answer a question you have or to give you some guidance for a decision you must make," I said. "I plan to lead you through a meditation like this at a later time. Because of the detachment that happens during meditation, you are more likely to get insights into what you are struggling with."

"When I have tried to meditate, I see colors and shapes inside my eyelids," Lisa said. "I assume I am not supposed to be concerned about that, right?"

"Correct," I responded. "If you paid attention to it, it would be the same as if you were watching things in your environment. You want to allow your awareness to go to a deeper level."

"Is prayer the same as meditating?" asked Al.

"Yes, essentially it is," I said. "When you pray, you ask for help from a higher power. When you meditate, you are doing the same thing, but without directly asking for it. The higher power whom you are addressing when you meditate is your spiritual Self.

"It really doesn't matter what you pray to. Whether you think of the higher power as being God or your spiritual Self, it is all really the same.

"There are some differences, however, between prayer and meditation. When you pray, if you ask for things, you are using your mind to think about them. This won't be as deep as when your mind is still. If you prolong the silence at the end of a prayer, that is meditation."

"What about altered states of consciousness?" Lisa asked. "Does this happen in meditation?"

"In meditation, you retain full consciousness of your physical body,"

I said. "You are not trying to alter your state of consciousness, such as to one that exists in deep hypnosis, daydreaming, or near-sleep. You want to be fully aware and conscious the entire time. An out-of-body experience is not what you are striving for, either.

Lisa had another question. "What should I do to prevent falling asleep while meditating?"

"I have heard various things about this," I answered. "One teacher said you have to pay attention when you are meditating so you recognize when you are getting sleepy. A suggestion was made to stand up while meditating if you need to keep from falling asleep. You can also do some chanting or breathing exercises to keep yourself awake.

"Another teacher explained if you try to meditate when you are tired, it will only be natural to fall asleep. She said not to worry about it and meditate at another time of day.

"I think the best advice I have heard is to meditate in the morning when you first awaken. Then you aren't tired or likely to be sleepy. Also, in the morning you are less tense because you're not yet wrapped up in the concerns of your day. It is easier to keep your mind clear.

"I would like to give you some additional guidelines as you start meditating. A regular schedule of meditation, at the same time and place, is desirable. You can start out simply. Then you won't get discouraged. If you meditate for just a few minutes a day, you will make progress. But meditating for twenty to thirty minutes is useful because it takes you awhile to relax and fully calm your mind. Then there is enough time left for a deeper experience.

"When you sit to meditate, make sure your spine is straight. This allows a smooth flow of energy throughout your body. If you lie down, you are likely to fall asleep. Start off with some deep, cleansing breaths, using your diaphragm to inhale deeply. Continue with abdominal breathing until you are relaxed. You don't have to sit cross-legged, but get into the habit of sitting with your legs and arms uncrossed. This allows your body to be most relaxed.

"You can start out meditating by remembering a moment of spiritual inspiration you have experienced. It may be from the harmony you feel in nature, or from an uplifting song at a church service. Recall the feeling of

Oneness. Realize this is within you all the time.

"Some people begin meditation by thinking of the qualities of a religious figure, such as the Virgin Mary, Christ, or a spiritual teacher. Others may listen to inspiring music, such as Beethoven's symphonies. Try different things to see what you harmonize with the best.

"The spiritual practices of nuns and monks in different religions vary, but they include a simple lifestyle incorporating prayer and meditation. There isn't anything mysterious about it. Some sing Latin chants, while others choose to remain silent all the time. There are many things you can do to get in touch with the spiritual part of yourself."

"Why are some monks silent?" asked Lisa.

"Silence serves the purpose of reducing the amount of activity in your everyday mind and emotions," I said. "When you don't interact with people, fewer things come into your mind, such as thoughts about conversations or disagreements with others. When your everyday mind is quiet, it is easier to pray. Silence helps the monks remain in a state of serenity."

Al inquired, "Earlier, you said everyone had received inspiration from their spiritual Self at one time or another. I think I know what you mean. I have two grandchildren whom I enjoy very much. Periodically, we spend a lot of time together. There have been times I have had so much love for them that I felt we could merge together and be one. Is this an example of the Oneness you speak of?"

"Yes, it is," I said. "Your relationship with them sounds wonderful."

Al continued, "I had another similar experience I wanted to ask you about. It was when I was with my hiking group on a trek in the mountains. We stopped for lunch as a group, but I wanted to take a short side trail to the top of this hill. So I went off alone. When I climbed to the top, I was amazed at what I could see. There were so many evergreen trees to look down upon, it seemed like I was looking at green velvet. The view of the other mountains was breathtaking. I had this expanded feeling within me. It took my breath away. I couldn't believe how beautiful it all was. Was I connecting to my spiritual Self then?"

"Yes, it sounds like you were," I told him. "I think everyone can relate to your experience. However, I wouldn't use the word 'connecting' to your spiritual Self. You are connected all the time, otherwise you wouldn't be alive. I would say you were 'open' to an awareness of your spiritual Self at that time. Thanks for sharing your experience. Does anyone else have a similar story?"

Lisa spoke. "I do. When I was a teenager, I went to our church camp for a week during the summer. Before every meal we would sing a song. This particular week, an excellent pianist was playing the accompaniment. One song was particularly jubilant. The pianist must have loved it, too, for she played it with such enthusiasm and inspiration. It was fantastic. As we sang the crescendos and the music swelled, I felt as though my heart would burst with joy. I didn't want to stop singing. I think I was singing from my spiritual Self, along with everyone else."

"I am sure you were," I said. "That is exactly what I am talking about. All the people at your church camp participated in making the atmosphere so joyous and elated that, according to the expression, it 'raised your spirits.' You raised your spiritual awareness to the level of your spiritual Self.

"Tonight, I plan to lead you through a meditation designed to open you to the spiritual aspect of nature. To begin with, sit in a relaxed position with your legs uncrossed and your hands resting comfortably in your lap. Close your eyes and take a few deep breaths. Fully exhale and let all the air out of your lungs. Relax as you breathe out and release the tension from your body."

The class members settled into their chairs and relaxed. A few stretched or rolled their shoulders.

"Let us feel harmony with the group."

Al tried to quiet his mind. He wasn't exactly sure what Sue meant about feeling harmony, but he decided it meant to feel accepting of the other people in the class.

"Let us feel harmony with nature. Picture a peaceful setting in a park or a forest."

Al knew exactly what he would picture in his mind. On one of his hikes, there had been a clearing that opened to a large grassy area surrounded by trees. He saw himself walking into it. The sun was shining and he imagined the air had the scent of flowers.

"Picture a tree. Imagine its roots deep into the ground. Feel yourself connected to that rootedness and stability."

Al didn't know what kind of tree to pick. He could imagine deciduous trees as well as evergreens. He decided to think of one of the large pine trees at the clearing's edge. He thought about how deep the roots must go and how they helped the tree withstand windy storms. When Sue asked him to feel connected to the tree's rootedness, he thought about how his wife always said he had his feet firmly planted on the ground.

"Notice the quietness of the tree. There is a stillness and peacefulness about it. Let that stillness be a part of you."

As Al pictured the tall, stately pine tree, he felt it represented inner strength and solemnity. He felt peaceful and quiet.

"Feel one with the tree. Be a part of the deeper Unity that underlies everything."

Al felt he was really getting into the meditation. A couple of times, he found his mind wandering. When this happened, he pictured the tree again. When he thought about the deeper Unity, he knew what it meant even without knowing how to put it into words. He felt a sense of satisfaction and peace.

"Experience the Oneness of all. Open to the silence and serenity that pervades everything."

When Al heard this, he figured he was on the right track. He realized his inner imagery of the trees in the clearing was a noiseless and soundless experience. He could see that being aware of the peacefulness was also done in silence. When he realized this was what meditation was all about, he settled into it even more.

"Let the peace and tranquillity you have experienced tonight be with you as you go through the week. When you are ready, come back to the room and open your eyes."

"What was the experience like for you?" I asked the group.

Al was really excited about what he had felt, but didn't want to speak up too quickly. He thought he would wait to see if someone else offered a comment. When no one did, he decided to share. "My meditation was really quite nice. Because I'm a hiker, I found it easy to think of a scene in nature. I pictured a clearing I am familiar with that has several stately evergreen trees. I felt peaceful and quiet. I think I even understood what you meant by 'experiencing the silence.' It is the silence surrounding your thoughts."

"That's a good way of phrasing it," I said.

"I know what you mean about the silence, Al," Lisa agreed. "I hadn't realized what Sue was referring to until just now. The silence seems to be the backdrop for everything."

"That's right," I said. "Silence is the stillness at your very core. It has been said that silence is 'God's language.' It is very powerful. In the Bible, Psalms 46:10 states, 'Be still, and know that I am God.' When you are open to your spiritual Self, your awareness is absolutely quiet. You don't recognize the silence with your ears. You perceive it with your heart."

Al made another comment. "I found my mind wandering several times during the meditation. It was amazing how easily thoughts came up. One moment I would be experiencing the sense of tranquillity, and the next moment I would be thinking about my wife. Before I knew it, I would slide into thinking about something ."

Lisa chimed in, "The same thing happened to me. I found it very hard to keep thinking about the nature scene. It seemed it was only a few seconds before my mind was off on a tangent. I guess it takes practice."

Ann was relieved when she heard these comments. She had thought something was wrong with her. She hadn't been able to keep from thinking about her daughters and what they were doing at home. She also went over the things she needed to do when she got back from the class. She was aware of how peaceful she felt, however, when everyone was meditating. It was very pleasant.

"Being interrupted by your thoughts is totally normal," I told the class. "This is due to the nature of your mind. Its function is to think. In a way, peace of mind does not exist. The peace is *beyond* your mind, because thoughts will always come up. The peace is in your awareness of it all.

"In a book called *The Voice of the Silence*, the activity of the mind is described in the words 'his thoughts become an army, and bear him off a captive slave.'[7] Your mind is always ready to start thinking about something. You may pick up on a memory that gets triggered. You may get absorbed in remembering a conversation or what you have read in a book.

To be aware only of the silence is like trying to concentrate only on your driving. When you drive, your mind can drift to other things because most of the time you don't encounter anything unusual. You know the way to your destination and you drive over familiar roads and routes. This is a perfect setup for your mind to wander."

"If it is so hard to do, what is the point?" Don probed. "I found it impossible to meditate."

"Did others of you experience this?" I asked.

One or two nodded their heads.

"I understand what you are saying," I assured them. "Don't worry about it now. In future classes, I will be introducing other ways for you to develop an awareness of the spiritual part of yourself. I don't want you to get frustrated. There are many pathways to spiritual development. They all end at the same goal. For example, helping someone in need can give you the same peace that prayer and meditation provide. We will be discussing other ways you can learn to express the qualities of your spiritual Self in classes to come.

"Let us shift now to consider another aspect of the 'Purpose of Life.' That is balance."

BALANCE

"As we discussed earlier, spiritual essence needs matter to make itself known. It needs to be rooted in the physical in order to have an existence. Without this, it could not grow and develop. You know what happens when a plant's root is destroyed — the plant dies. There can be no plant without a root. The same is true with spirit. It cannot evolve without matter. Life on our planet provides consciousness as a vehicle for this.

"Spirit and matter are necessary for each other. They are like two sides of the same coin. They cannot be separated. Each side can be known only by the presence of the other. Spirit provides the illumination for matter to be perceived, such as through your intelligence, and matter provides the vehicle of perception, as in your physical brain and senses.

"Just as matter serves a purpose for spirit, the same holds true with many seemingly negative things in life, such as evil, hatred, and suffering.

They each serve a purpose for their counterpart."

"How can that be? They seem so unnecessary," said Jane.

"They provide you with experiences that teach you what it feels like to be the target of hatred and animosity," I responded. "You learn about the effects of harm done to you, the same way you learn what it feels like to be shown love. This teaches you how to treat others. Negative experiences give you the ability to understand why the positive is better."

"It sounds like you are saying there is a purpose to suffering. Is that so?" Lisa asked.

"Yes, out of suffering comes knowledge," I said. "By knowing evil, the aspiration for good has meaning. By experiencing hatred, you can know what it means to love. Suffering allows you to perceive and appreciate happiness, as well as to desire it for others.

"The existence of evil, or non-love, is the necessary counterpart of good. If evil did not exist, good would not be apparent. It wouldn't be known. It would simply be. Each is created out of knowledge of the other. You understand why evil is undesirable from its contrast to good. This is what is meant by the expression 'Only during the dark of night can you see the stars.'

"The same is true with other desirable qualities, such as peacefulness, harmony, contentment, and friendship. Without their opposites, you would not be able to fully realize their natures. The quality of each one is appreciated and understood by knowing its negative side.

"Can you come up with some examples which demonstrate this?" I asked the class.

Al said, "I think the presence of war in the world eventually teaches people the things they are fighting over, such as land, boundaries, or religious beliefs, are meaningless if you can't feel safe and live in peace."

"Great example! How about another?" I asked.

There was silence for awhile. Reluctantly, Anne took a breath and spoke up. "This makes me think of how good I feel when our family is enjoying each other and not fighting."

"I know what you mean," I said. "Argument provides you with a true appreciation for getting along and living harmoniously. Anyone else?"

"I sure am thankful for my health whenever I get sick," Jane remarked.

"I usually take it for granted. Only when I feel lousy do I really know how good it is to feel healthy."

"Yes, that happens to me, too," I said. "So, you can see by these examples how the knowledge of any two opposites gives you valuable information about how to regulate and moderate your life. The opposites complement one other. If one is eliminated, the other becomes destructive. Together, they produce a balance. Plants would die if they only had sunshine without the darkness of night. The same principle is true with your body's need for activity, as well as rest. It would deteriorate without sleep or be lethargic without exercise.

"Too much of anything causes problems. If you fill your cup too full, it will spill. If you work too hard, you will become exhausted. Care too much about other people's approval, and you give away your freedom. These all emphasize that when something is out of balance, there are negative consequences in your life.

"As you go about your day-to-day life, your physical body also is constantly seeking equilibrium. If you don't eat or drink enough, you become hungry or thirsty. If you stay up too late, the next day you feel tired. If you exercise too much, your muscles become sore. All your body's responses to maintain balance are automatic.

"The same is true with your vehicles of consciousness. They harmonize well together when they, too, are in balance. As you live in the world, you simultaneously use your physical, emotional, mental, and spiritual bodies. You need them all. If one is used to excess, the rest are adversely affected.

"For example, if you are consumed by worry, it will stress your physical body and make you vulnerable to illness and exhaustion. Your sense of spiritual unity is also forgotten. Taking another example, if you pray all the time, you may neglect your household responsibilities, thereby giving your family, and ultimately you, emotional turmoil. Balance is important, so that each aspect of your nature is in harmony with every other.

"When something is out of balance, you have to deal with the negative results of your behavior. This gives you an opportunity to learn from your actions. An undesirable outcome provides you with a concrete experience so you really know why one course of action is better than another.

The 'bad' consequences allow you to grow. This is true for every opposite. They all serve the same purpose.

"The word 'polarity' means 'the presence of opposites.' Let's make a list of all the opposites you can think of."

I took out my large writing tablet and wrote "Polarities" at the top. The class brainstormed ideas which I made into a list. Some of the highlights were:

POLARITIES

good	bad
awake	asleep
summer	winter
exercise	rest
happy	sad
cold	hot
male	female
birth	death

"These opposites are present throughout life. They are depicted by the Chinese yin/yang symbol. It represents life, which has a balance of everything.

"During the course of your existence, you encounter things that are both positive and negative. They happen continually. This is portrayed by the light and dark portions of the symbol. Neither side can be known without the other. Each part rounds out your knowledge. Together they complete the picture, which is depicted by the symbol's circular shape. The circle also stands for the Unity from which everything arises.

"There are many benefits to the opposites in life. Because they complement each other, they enhance and improve everything you experience. For example, the existence of the two sexes of male and female provide interest, pleasure, and a more complete life experience. The change of season brings variety to the environment. Strenuous work is balanced by relaxation. Interacting with others works well in combination with time spent alone for introspection and reflection. You feel better when your life is in balance. There is a greater sense of well being."

"Are life and death also necessary for each other?" asked Al.

"Yes," I said, "they are essential for evolution and growth. Death is necessary so that you may rest from the toils of life and live in your spirit. In turn, life is longed for by spiritual essence as it seeks to feel itself alive once again on the physical plane. Nothing lasts. Change always occurs. One naturally resolves itself into the other.

"In Zen Buddhism, it is said that being alive on the physical plane is like being in a house that is on fire. You can last only so long. Life is consuming. It is hard on your body and takes its toll. Death provides a chance to start life over with new vitality and vigor. This liveliness is evident in the energy of children and young adults.

"The cycles of change go on continually and balance out over time. They never stop. One aspect of change gradually fades into the next phase. This is what is meant by the expression 'the end is the beginning and the beginning is the end.' An example of this is the change of the tides. When the tide has finished coming in, the ebb tide takes its place and the water recedes. One phase ends to let the next one begin.

"Each phase of the cycle of change has its purpose. Each contributes to the overall state of equilibrium necessary for life to flourish. This is demonstrated by the four seasons. Spring and summer bring sunshine and growth after the darkness of winter. Fall turns plants to seed. Winter provides a time for dormancy.

"The changing cycles can be seen in the course of an individual's life. In your personal life, you have periods when you are out in the world, interacting and making new relationships. This is demonstrated when you become independent from your parents and begin working at a vocation. At other times, you spend more time at home with projects or activities there. An example is when a couple buys a house or begins a family.

"This process is spoken about in the Bible, in Ecclesiastes 3:1–8:

> "To everything there is a season, and a time to every purpose under the heaven. A time to be born, and a time to die; a time to plant, and a time to pluck up that which is planted; a time to kill, and a time to heal; a time to break

down, and a time to build up; a time to weep and a time
to laugh; a time to mourn, and a time to dance; a time to
cast away stones and a time to gather stones together; a
time to embrace, and a time to refrain from embracing;
a time to get, and a time to lose; a time to keep, and a
time to cast away; a time to rend and a time to sew; a
time to keep silence, and a time to speak; a time to love,
and a time to hate; a time of war and a time of peace.

"There are many examples of growth that happen after a period of
suffering. Compromise and reconciliation come from differences and disagreement. Restoration of your sense of self and greater confidence come
from resolving grief and despair. Suffering provides a chance to develop
sympathy for others, because you truly know from experience what someone else is going through.

"The difficult times in your life provide valuable lessons for you. John
Vance Cheney poetically wrote about this in the words, 'The soul would
have no rainbow had the eyes no tears.' 'Tears' come with the pain of loss
and other strife in your life. Overcoming them allows the rainbow of your
soul to shine through.

"In nature as well, something good develops out of every seemingly
negative thing. For example, pearls come from sand irritating oysters. Pressure and heat produce diamonds. Volcanoes in the ocean produce new
islands.

"Destruction is necessary for regeneration. Flowers spring from dirt
and decaying leaves. Forest fires clear the land of dead wood and scrub
plants to make way for flourishing new growth.

"So, relating this subject back to 'The Purpose of Life,' you can see
each event in your life is one piece that fits into the larger whole. Stepping
back and looking at the big picture allows you to see how you gain from
disappointments and setbacks. All the circumstances and events that take
place contribute to your evolution and growth.

"We've had a good discussion this evening. Since it is late, let's adjourn. Good luck as you try meditating this next week."

NOTES

1. Alcyone aka J. Krishnamurti, *At the Feet of the Master* (Madras, India: The Theosophical Publishing House, 1910), p. 70.
2. Charles W. Leadbeater, *A Textbook of Theosophy* (Madras, India: The Theosophical Publishing House, 1912), p. 98.
3. B.W. Huntsman, ed., *Wisdom Is One* (London: Pitman Press, 1947), p. 39.
4. Annie Besant and Charles W. Leadbeater, *Talks On the Path of Occultism*, Volume I (Madras, India: The Theosophical Publishing House, 1926), pp. 6–7.
5. Annie Besant, trans., The Bhagavad-Gita (Madras, India: The Theosophical Publishing House, 1953), p. 76.
6. Awo Fa'lokun Fatunmbi, *Iba'se Orisa* (New York: Original Publications, 1994), p. 16.
7. Helena Petrovna Blavatsky, *The Voice of the Silence* (Madras, India: The Theosophical Publishing House, 1968), p. 28.

Karma

"One of the most common concepts among all religions and philosophies of life is the subject of karma. You probably have heard the term, but may not understand what it means. It is really quite simple.

"Karma comes from the Sanskrit language of ancient India. Literally, it means 'to act.' Knowing the exact meaning of the word, however, doesn't give you a clear understanding of what karma represents. Karma refers to a principle of life that has a greater significance. It represents the law of cause and effect.

"This may sound rather technical, but it will become clear with some examples. The law of cause and effect means that for every cause, which means something that is done, there is an effect, or the result of that action. Take the example of hitting a golf ball. Hitting the ball is the cause. The effect of that action is the ball flying through the air. If you hit the golf ball hard, it will travel far. If you hit it gently, it will move only a few feet. Karma will vary depending upon the intensity of your initial action. The power of karma differs with each circumstance.

"Another example of karma is how you treat other people. If you are rude to someone, he probably will not like you and may treat you the same way in return. Your action of being rude is the cause. The karma is the other person's dislike and the same treatment back to you.

"This example shows the rebound effect. Karma rebounds back to where it came from. In this case, it rebounds to the person who was rude first.

"Sometimes, there is a series of rude or angry behaviors between people, with each incident causing another insult. There may be no obvious starting point. An ongoing feud is an example of this. This can occur in a marriage or between close family members.

"How you act toward others will come back to you. It is reflected in the expressions 'What goes around, comes around' and 'You reap what you sow.'

"Karma is a basic law of the universe. It is described in a physics class when a teacher explains the law of action and reaction. This states that for every action, there is an equal and opposite reaction. If you pull a pendulum to one side, it will swing back toward the opposite side."

I removed a necklace from around my neck and held it with the pendant hanging at the bottom. I then pulled the pendant to one side and released it, allowing it to swing back and forth. "This demonstrates karma. It shows how the necklace rebounds back to the side where it was first pulled.

"Karma also applies to your thoughts and feelings. At the emotional level, if you don't like someone, that person will probably be able to sense it, even if you don't say anything. It is evident from your mood and the expression on your face. This acts as a cause. The result, or the karma, is the other person feeling ill at ease around you. He or she may want to avoid you. It can also create an unpleasant and stiff atmosphere for others nearby.

"Let me give you another example of karma at the mental level. If you are frequently thinking about ways you feel inadequate, the result will be that you lose self-esteem and trust in yourself. Repeatedly thinking about something gives it more energy. This acts as a 'cause.' It results in the growth of your lack of confidence.

"Negative thinking, in turn, may prevent you from going out and interacting with others. This can deprive you of positive interactions which not only are fun, but also give you support and encouragement. It leaves the door open for your mood to spiral downward and make you feel even worse. The karmic effects of your actions can branch out and affect you in several ways."

Al spoke up. "You hear about 'good' karma. Does this mean that some karma is negative and some is positive?"

"Good question," I said. "Karma is neither good nor bad. It is neutral. It is often thought that karma refers to unpleasant events, but karma results from 'good' actions, as well.

"For example, if you are helpful to someone, that person will respond with gratitude and kindness. They are also more likely to go on to help someone else who is in need.

"In addition, your helpful behavior can act as a model for others, who may also pitch in to help those in need. Finally, the result of your helping others may be that someone will probably help you in the future, if you are ever in need."

"Why does karma exist in the first place?" Don asked.

THE PURPOSE OF KARMA

"Karma exists to restore balance," I said. "If you recall our discussion last week, we looked at how nature, as well as the entire physical world, is continuously seeking equilibrium. It is an ongoing process and a natural part of life. Karma does the same thing. It maintains balance by providing the proper consequence for every action you take. This applies to non-physical actions, such as your motivations and intentions, as well as physical behaviors.

"However, the ultimate purpose of karma is to teach. It does this by providing you with experiences from which you learn about the effects of what you do. I'm sure you have all heard of the Golden Rule. It says you should 'do unto others as you would have others do unto you.' It is difficult to live by this rule unless you have experienced, firsthand, the pain from being treated poorly. Then you truly know what it feels like and probably won't do the same to someone else.

"Experience is the best teacher for you to really know if something is true. Even if a child is told that fire is hot, he will still try to feel it. Only by feeling the heat does he know it and believe it.

"Karma develops your character. It helps you grow and develop positive characteristics, such as patience and compassion.

"Let us look at an example. If you have been impatient or unkind with someone, he or she will probably treat you that way in return. The discomfort you experience teaches you about patience and kindness, because that is the way you would want to be treated.

"The suffering from karma isn't meant to be cruel. Its purpose is to give you a similar experience so you can learn what it is like."

"Does karma end once the effect is over?" Jim asked.

"Yes," I said. "Once karma is released, the energy is neutralized. You have paid your debt, so to speak, and are in the clear. But it is important to realize the effect of your actions, that is, the karma of your actions extends outward with no end. It is similar to throwing a rock into a pond. The ripples move outward in a circle and become weaker the farther they are from the rock. But, in a sense, they never end.

"Even another set of ripples caused by a second rock doesn't necessarily eliminate the first set. They cross each other and keep going. Eventually, every part of the pond is affected by the waves from the rock, even if only in a subtle way. Being aware of this, you can see that being kind and helpful is the type of energy you would want going out everywhere."

"Does karma happen right away?" asked Al.

"Not always," I said. "The energy of karma may accumulate, like electrical energy stored in a battery. When the time is right, the karmic energy is released. It may be felt in a different way, but the energy will always be released.

"Karma accumulates because its effects may need to be withheld until the time is right for you to get the most from the experience. Remember, the purpose of karma is to teach. It will be released when you can best learn the qualities you need to develop.

"An example of this is a builder who uses poor-quality materials to build houses. He may be able to sell several homes and feel successful. But just as he is living well off his profits, he is confronted by a lawsuit, brought by several homeowners, that wipes him out financially. In this case, the builder needs the strong impact of a lawsuit from which to learn."

THE TYPES OF KARMA

"There are different types of karma. One is immediate karma and another is time-delayed. Immediate karma is the result of current actions in your life. If you touch a hot iron, your hand will get burned.

"Time-delayed karma is the result of your actions in the past. If you don't take out the garbage for a week, it will start to smell.

"Let me give you another illustration of time-delayed karma. If you steal something, but get away with it, the karma will still be there. It may seem like everything is fine, but you will reap the effects of your actions in some way in the future. One outcome may be that someone steals something from you. If that doesn't happen, you may be deprived of something that is rightfully yours. You never know how it will play out. The only sure thing is the results of your actions will always come back to you.

"Another type of karma, which affects large numbers of people, is called group or collective karma. An example of this is when an entire population is affected by some event, such as a war or a famine. These types of events are said to be the result of karma.

"Yet another type of karma is 'piled-up' karma. This is the entire amount of karma a person has built up during all of his evolution. This needs to be worked out over a series of lifetimes. Usually, the karma in this category is from doing harmful or selfish things. This is only natural, however. When a person is first evolving, he is more primitive in his behavior, operating out of a survival instinct rather than from reason. He is more selfish and likely to commit acts to benefit himself, but at a cost to others, such as taking someone else's food. He may have even murdered someone to get his way.

"Remember, this is done out of ignorance. He has no understanding of the degree he affects others. They are looked on impersonally, like trees or rocks. This is a stage of development and is important in the whole scheme of things. Evolution can't occur any other way. Just as crawling is necessary before you can walk, selfish behavior is necessary before unselfishness is learned."

"Why might karma take several lifetimes to resolve itself?" asked Jane. "Why not in just one lifetime, or all at once?"

"If a great accumulation of karma were all released in one lifetime," I said, "the effects would be crushing, rather than providing an opportunity for growth. Because the purpose of karma is to teach, karma is dispensed gradually in order for people to learn from their actions, but not to overwhelm them. Only a certain amount is allocated for each lifetime."

"Is there any order or pattern to how karma is released? For instance, is it more difficult at the beginning of a person's evolution and easier at the end?" asked Jane.

"No," I answered, "there is no set pattern in the way that karma is distributed. It is unique for each person's circumstances. It is constantly changing as the conditions in life change."

"How is karma determined?" Al inquired.

"Karma, being a natural law, has forces working at the higher planes which do this naturally," I said. "An 'intelligence,' so to speak, decides the general conditions of life or certain, specific life events an individual will have. This is not the intelligence from a person or a group of people. The intelligence is only a metaphor for the power and wisdom of the entire universe, of which karma is a part."

"Are events in life predetermined?" Al asked.

"No, your fate is not cast in concrete. It may seem there is no choice in life and that matters are out of your hands. Definitely, certain conditions are set before you are born, such as the genetics of your body or the environment you are born into. Even so, you have free will to make choices in how you think and behave. You have the power to choose your reactions to conditions you can't control. You can choose how you accept 'the way the cookie crumbles.' "

"What is the best way to handle karma?" Jim asked.

"I think your question is about handling 'negative' karma," I said. " 'Good' karma gives you opportunities and favorable circumstances you naturally take advantage of. 'Bad' karma presents you with roadblocks on your way throughout life. The roadblocks are setbacks, disappointments, and other difficulties.

"Problems don't have to overwhelm you. Make adjustments and rethink your position. Then you will be led by reason, rather than feelings of failure or self-pity. If you accept the circumstances, you will find a way to work around them.

"You will also allow karma to be balanced out, or 'burned up,' as some say. So often you hear it said that any changes people are forced to make because of a disappointment turn out in the end to be for the better.

"Accepting the conditions of life you can't control allows you to see the positive aspects of your situation. You see the glass half-full, rather than half-empty. You also realize things could have been much worse. My grandmother always used to say:

"From the day you are born
"Until they carry you away in a hearse,
"For whatever you've got,
"There is always something worse."

"In church last Sunday," Al said, "our minister spoke about this very subject. He said we should be grateful for whatever happens in life, whether it is good or bad, because it has been sent as a guide from beyond, or as a pointer from God."

Lisa commented, "I like the way that is put. If a disappointing circumstance can be thought of as a guide for you stay on the right track, it takes away the 'awfulness' of the situation, particularly if you think of it as being the start of something better."

"That's true," I said. "However, sometimes circumstances are difficult to handle and you need help to get you through. This is a time for therapy. Therapy can assist you in understanding your feelings, which can be overpowering. It helps lessen your confusion so you can reason things through. It can lift depression and help you let go of old hurts to move to a state of forgiveness.

Lisa asked, "Does it work for how you feel about your parents?"

"Yes," I said, "because when people do hurtful things, it is caused by ignorance. This is true for parents, as well. They are not perfect. To a child, they seem all-powerful and all-knowing. But the parents who raised them, your grandparents, weren't perfect either. In all likelihood, your parents were just repeating the same mistakes their parents made.

"Parents can hurt their children with careless remarks. They can condition them to feel a certain way about themselves. They can set the stage for a child to draw faulty conclusions about himself which are totally wrong, such as 'my parents don't love me, so there must be something wrong with me.'

"Again, therapy helps you uncover these conclusions, as well as the conditioning that caused them, so you can begin to free yourself from their influence. It allows you to grieve over past wrongs and release the pain and hurt. You may be able to prevent making the same mistakes with your own children."

"I know this was the case with my dad," Jane related. "He was treated badly by his father, so when it came to raising me, he didn't know how to be anything but gruff. I saw Sue at the time of my divorce and dealt with some of the pain from my childhood then."

CAN KARMA BE CHANGED?

"Is there any way to change karma?" asked Jim.

"Yes, to an extent," I said. "You can't change it totally, but you can influence it. Karma can be modified, but it follows the laws of physics, nonetheless. You learn in science class that the effect of any action or force can be modified by applying a force from another direction. If you hit a golf ball, which is a force from one direction, and the wind is blowing toward you, which is a force from another direction, the golf ball won't travel as far as it would if the air were still.

"Let us look at another example. If you throw a ball up into the air, you know it will come down. Suppose you throw the ball in an area where there are people. The karma from your action may be someone getting hit.

"Since you don't want to hurt anyone, you can take some actions to modify the karma. You can't change the fact that gravity will bring the ball down, but you can call out to people to get out of the way. You can also reach up and try to catch the ball or deflect it in another direction. Finally, you can apologize to people and ease their anger, which is another karmic result from your ball-throwing."

"Can this be applied to negative karma in general?" Lisa asked.

"Yes, it can," I said. "First of all, you know you probably have a certain amount of 'piled-up' negative karma from past actions that have hurt others. This is only natural in the course of your evolution. The negative karma is generally caused by selfishness. You may have been selfish over tangible things, such as food or money, or by thinking only of yourself and hurting someone's feelings.

"Therefore, because the force that causes negative karma is selfishness, you can counteract it by applying an equal but opposite force, which is kindness and unselfishness. The more you feel, think, and perform unselfish and kindly acts toward others, the more you ease your burden of negative karma.

"By the way, this also means that you should be kind to yourself, without using put-downs or thinking you are unworthy or unacceptable."

"I can relate to what you are saying," said Al. "When I am kind and caring to my wife, things in general seem to go better. She is more caring back to me and it seems to perpetuate itself."

"Yes, going out of your way for someone elicits the same kind of response in return," I said. "Even if you merely desire to be good and kind to others, you will start to act that way as a result of your desire.

"One's inner motivation has a powerful effect, because it comes from spiritual will, which is inexhaustible. Your inner motivation influences your thoughts, which precede any action. Generally, you act in the same manner that you think. So if you carefully monitor the content of your thinking, you will dramatically affect your behavior.

"To correct tougher problems, such as losing your temper, you may need to use behavior modification and employ specific anger management techniques. But gradually, your behavior will change.

"Spiritual teachers say a little energy in a positive direction, such as through love and understanding, counterbalances a greater amount of negativity and hate. This means being kind and patient is an effective way to neutralize an even greater amount of negative energy from another person."

"How does that work?" asked Don. "It seems hard to believe."

Al chimed in, "Yet it follows what Christ said about love."

"That's true," I said. "It works because of the nature of the higher planes of consciousness. Remember, the energy of unselfishness expresses itself through very rapid vibrations. It has a force that is more penetrating and enduring than selfishness and hatred, which is characterized by slower and coarser vibrations. So, courtesy and congeniality are more powerful and actually soften and dissipate anger and fear.

"If you are kind and patient with someone in a chance encounter at the supermarket, you will see the effects of kindness calming the person immediately.

"If you have had a long-lasting conflict with someone in your family, it may take a little time before you see the result. But if you suppress yourself from returning any negative remarks made to you, you set forces in motion that will contribute to a reconciliation.

"The karma from attempts at peacemaking is like a seed in the ground lying dormant before it sprouts. Eventually the plant will grow, mature, and produce a harvest. In time, your efforts will pay off.

"Suppose you have had a long-standing disagreement with your sister. If you change your own resentment into feelings of goodwill toward her, over time this will ease the tension between you.

"There are several reasons why this occurs. First of all, you change your own mental state about your sister, which neutralizes your reactions to her. Secondly, because you influence how your sister acts toward you by what you expect of her, you subtly influence her to show her goodness, which is inherent in all people. Finally, you feel better throughout the entire process, because when there is a sense of goodwill in yourself, your mood is lighter and you feel better."

"I have a question about interfering with someone's karma," Al said. "Should you go ahead and help someone who is in trouble, even if it changes his karma?"

"Yes," I said, "generally, you should offer your assistance to anyone who can use your help. Never hold back from helping another out of fear you are interfering with their karma. Karma is constantly being adjusted as conditions in life change. After all, it may have been that person's karma to be helped by you."

"Does karma end when a person dies?" Jane asked.

"No, karma carries over from lifetime to lifetime," I answered. "Death does not cancel karma, any more than moving to a new city cancels the debts you incurred in the previous one. Karma will be interwoven into the circumstances of your next life. You always meet the consequences of your deeds. This is taught in *The Rubaiyat of Omar Khayyam.*

> "The Moving Finger writes; and, having writ,
> "Moves on: nor all your Piety nor Wit
> "Shall lure it back to cancel half a Line,
> "Nor all your Tears wash out a Word of it.'

"It is important to understand that karma itself does not create anything. You are the one who plans and creates. Each action or decision you make has consequences, no matter how great or small. The responsibility is yours."

"When you describe this," commented Al, "it makes me think about the decisions people make to build homes at the edge of a river or next to the ocean where flooding is likely to occur. The river is not at fault if someone's home is ruined."

"You're right," I said. "The lesson here is to live in harmony with all that exists. This includes nature, as well as human beings.

"I'd like to talk about another aspect of karma. Spiritual teachers say that karma provides a reward for every suffering, the same way that nature has an antidote for every poison. With every disappointment, new opportunities open up. With every loss, something is gained.

"Take the example of a man who works too hard and has a heart attack. In order to live in a more healthy manner, he has to make changes in his lifestyle. These may be difficult to do, but in the long run, they allow him to enjoy more free time or retire early.

"Another example is the story of a woman whose husband and child die in a car accident. She has to resolve tremendous grief, but develops more self-reliance and a stronger bond with her surviving children."

"That happened to one of the families in our church," Al shared. "The husband was killed at work shortly after one of their children died from a long struggle with leukemia. The wife came through the tragedy with a sense of strength she never knew she had. She said she always feared this kind of thing, but when it happened she found she could handle it."

"Good for her," I said. "This principle of something good coming from negative events is depicted in the Chinese ideogram representing 'crisis.' I'm sure you all have seen Chinese characters. They can stand for individual words or an entire concept.

"The meaning of the Chinese symbol for 'crisis' is two-fold. It represents both 'danger' and 'opportunity.' The 'danger' from a crisis is the threat to you, your family, or your way of life. Something you value is at risk and may be destroyed. The 'opportunity' represents the potential for positive change resulting from the crisis. Keeping this in mind can help you anticipate the ways your life will improve as a result of change that is imposed on you.

"Karma is the principle behind the way parents teach children about harmonious behavior in a family. Parents give positive consequences for behavior they want to develop, such as praising a child who shares his toys. They determine negative consequences for behavior they want to change, such as sending a child to his room as a 'time-out' for fighting. Parents select the karma for the behavior they want to see or not see in their children."

Al raised a question. "What about people we have known in past lifetimes? Is there any way to tell whether we have karma to work out with them?"

"I have heard it said if you want to know the people you have past karma with, all you need to do is look at your family and close associates, such as friends or work partners," I responded. "If you have loving relationships now, you probably had similar ones in the past. If you have problems getting along, this is most likely a continuation of strife you had in a former lifetime. The circumstances were different then, but a resolution may never have been found.

"However, it doesn't matter what happened in the past. What is important is the opportunity you have now to resolve conflicts in your life."

"What should you do in a case where a fight goes on and on?" inquired Lisa. "Is it useful to give in to stop arguments from going on indefinitely?"

I decided to turn this question over to the class.

Jim spoke up first. "I think it would be beneficial to do that. I know any time I have made an effort to resolve a conflict with someone I don't get along with, I am always glad I did. The problems may not be over, but I feel good I tried."

Lisa shook her head. "That's easier said than done," she countered. "What do you do with someone who won't work with you? My sister seems to want to fight and hold on to her resentments forever. I can't seem to get anywhere with her."

"Maybe you should look at why you can't get along with her," countered Don.

"What do you mean?" Lisa said.

"If you can't get along," Don replied, "don't blame your sister. She can't fight alone. Look at yourself."

Jane chimed in, "I think there are people who jump at the chance to fight with someone. But that doesn't mean you have to fight back."

"It seems if you fight," Jim offered, "you are only making more 'negative' karma, no matter if you were the one who started it or not."

"This is not an easy subject," I said. "There are no simple answers. It all contributes to your learning. The key is to look at your reactions to see if they are effective or not. If they aren't, you may want to try a different approach."

"Do animals make karma?" Al asked.

"Yes, the principle of karma works for animals, too," I said. "For example, if a gorilla displays antisocial behavior, the other gorillas banish him from the group. He may be accepted back if his behavior changes. However, with animals, there is little conscious choice about what they do. They operate mainly on instinct. Because of this, karma is not the same teacher as it is to human beings.

"People also affect the karma of animals. If the owner of a dog treats it with kindness and understanding, it influences the development of the dog's awareness of people's moods. The animal becomes more sensitive and caring to his owner. If a dog is trained to be on guard and ready to attack, it doesn't have a chance to develop patience or sensitivity."

"What about a young child dying of cancer? Is that the result of karma?" Lisa asked.

"That is a complicated question," I said. "Karma probably is involved, as it is with everything in life. This particular example is difficult to understand from our limited perspective. We can't see the past lives of the child and the parents in order to know how the events of one lifetime fit in with the whole. It is not possible for us to understand the unique way it contributes to the child's and the parents' evolution.

"This kind of situation is accepted as a part of life. Christians may say circumstances like this are 'God's will.' This refers to the higher power that guides the unfolding of events and conditions in our world.

"Reincarnation helps you understand how karma works. Consider each lifetime as a single bead on a necklace. Each bead has a series of beads preceding it and following it. Previous lifetimes influence circumstances in the 'beads' or the lifetimes that follow.

"The influence which determines the environmental factors in the next life or 'bead' is karma. If you look at one bead alone, there may seem to be inequities in that one situation. But if you look at the entire 'necklace' of lifetimes, you will understand the particular circumstances in one life."

KARMA IN THE BIBLE

"Are there references to karma in the Bible?" Al asked.

"Yes, there are quite a few," I said. "Some of them are:

"Galatians 6:7, 'Be not deceived; God is not mocked: for whatsoever a man soweth, that shall he also reap. For he that soweth to his flesh shall of the flesh reap corruption: but he that soweth to the Spirit shall of the Spirit reap life everlasting';

"Job 4:8, 'They that plow iniquity and sow trouble, reap the same';

"Isaiah 3:10, 'Say ye of the righteous, that it shall be well with him: for they shall eat the fruit of their doings';

"Matthew 7:1–2, 'Judge not, that ye be not judged. For with what judgment ye judge, ye shall be judged: and with what measure ye mete, it shall be measured to you again';

"Revelation 13:9, 'If any man hath an ear, let him hear! He that leadeth into captivity, shall go into captivity: He that killeth with the sword must be killed with the sword.' "

Lisa brought up a question about the Bible verse, Deuteronomy 19:31, which says, "Eye for eye, tooth for tooth, hand for hand, foot for foot." She wondered whether it represented karma.

"This verse is similar to the previous quote in Revelation 13:9," I said. "It means the law of karma, or retribution, is fair and not meant to punish or exact a penalty on anyone. It indicates you will have a consequence that is equal to your original action and nothing more.

"Biblical scholars might disagree on the interpretation of the verse, but this is what it is commonly thought to mean. The Bible is not encouraging you to knock someone's teeth out because they do it to you. That would only create more karma."

"If you did that," Al stated, "it would go against Christ's teaching about turning the other cheek to someone who hits you. He taught that you should forgive and forget."

Jim offered, "The Bible also says in Romans 12:19, 'Vengeance is mine: I will repay, saith the Lord.' I think this means we are not supposed to worry about getting even with people. That can be left to God, or to karma."

"Are there teachings about karma in other traditions?" Al asked.

"Yes, the various religions of the world say many things about karma," I said. "The word 'karma' comes from Hinduism, but other philosophies teach the same concept. One saying about karma from the Yoruba religion of Africa is 'The person who harms others, when he has been harmed, is unable to settle a dispute.'[1] From this example, you can see that the karma from harming someone is that you, in turn, will be harmed and unable to get help from the authorities.

"Another common saying about karma is also stated in the Yoruba religion. It says, 'The person who makes their own bed sleeps in it.'[2] I'm sure you have all heard this analogy. It means you are responsible for whatever happens in your life. This is the 'bed' you lie in. You have to sleep in it until you remake your life into one that you want.

"An adage I have heard attributed to the Jewish tradition warns you to be careful in what you say. 'If your tongue turns into a knife, it will cut off your lips.' This means if you speak in ways that cut into people like a knife, your thoughtlessness will come back to you in a similar manner.

"To counteract this, a piece of advice from my grandmother tells you, 'Do not sever your heart from your tongue.' If you speak in unkind ways, you cut yourself off from your 'heart.' Your heart, or your compassion, will help keep you from hurting someone else.

"Yet another old adage describes the workings of karma. 'Ashes fly back into the face of he who throws them.' The 'ashes' are the results of your deeds."

"I love all those sayings," exclaimed Lisa. "They are so true!"

"What about the views of Muslims on karma? Do they have similar teachings?" Al asked.

"Yes," I said, "the holy scriptures of the Islamic religion, the Koran, have several verses that are relevant to karma. Verse 17:7 says, 'If you do good, you do good for your own selves, and if you do evil, you do it against yourselves.' Verse 53:31 says, 'Allah may requite those who do evil with that which they have done and reward those who do good, with what is best.'

"I'd like to share two other quotes before we move on. A passage in the Tibetan Book of the Dead 2:1 reads, 'That thou are suffering so cometh from thine own karma; it is not due to anyone else's: it is thine own karma.'

"Finally, from Sikhism, which is a religion similar to Hinduism, it states in the Trilochan 6:80, 'Thy woe and weal are according to thine acts.'

"These quotes should give you a sense of the wide range of teachings about karma throughout the world."

"Let's take a break now before we go on to the next topic."

MANTRAS

"Some of you expressed in last week's class that you were having a hard time with meditation. This next discussion may be useful to you. I'd like to acquaint you with the subject of mantras.

"You are aware that the focus of this class is to teach you about the nature of your personal self and how to rise above it to open to your spiritual Self. One of the ways to do this is through meditation.

"Meditation is difficult because of interfering thoughts. To counteract this, and to help you calm your mind and emotions, you can chant a mantra.

"A mantra is a word or phrase used to invoke spiritual energy in the person reciting it. You simply repeat it over and over again. Not only does it help you relax and empty your mind of its normal thinking, but it also opens you up to the spiritual part of yourself.

"The word 'mantra' is from Sanskrit, and comes from the root 'man,' which means 'mind,' and 'tra,' which means 'instrument.' A mantra is an instrument for the mind. You use it to elicit a state of calm that allows you to be more in tune with your spiritual Self.

"Chanting a mantra uses the influence of sound. Sound has a powerful effect on all living creatures, animals as well as humans. The energy of sound stimulates your feelings and elicits a reaction that is unique to the type of sound you hear. For example, if you hear monks singing a Gregorian chant, you feel differently than when you hear an audience yelling at a boxing match.

"One reason why reactions vary is due to the nature of sound. The energy of sound is in the form of vibrations. Lower-pitched sounds have slower vibrations. Higher-pitched sounds have faster vibrations. Similarly, the energy of your emotional and mental bodies also is in the form of vibrations. Moods that are depressed or irritated have denser and slower vibrations than lighter moods of happiness and spiritual joy.

"Listening to a particular type of sound will influence you to have a similar response in your emotional and mental bodies. For example, the sound of a loud engine or the roar of a lion will influence you to experience the coarser vibrations associated with agitation or fear.

"Soft, high-pitched sounds, such as the sound of a mother singing to her baby, are made of more delicate vibrations. These sounds produce a gentle and soothing effect.

"When you hear a sound, the emotional body reacts immediately. Because the emotional body is fluid, the effect of a sudden, startling sound that comes on quickly will also dissipate quickly. You may be startled by the sound of someone dropping a book, but you can quickly adjust back to your normal state.

"If a sound is repeated over a long period of time, its influence on the emotional body will increase and become stronger. The sustained sound of hammering can make you irritable, while the sound of a mother humming lullabies can put a baby to sleep."

Al asked, "I have heard Tibetan monks chanting, and their voices are extremely low. Does this matter?"

"No," I said. "The high or low pitch of the mantra is not as important as the evenness of the tone. Loud, chaotic sounds are disturbing, whereas the repetition of a mantra is gentle. It is uniform and orderly. It contributes to a feeling of harmony. This helps your emotional body become steady and calm, allowing you to be more in tune with your spiritual Self.

"Repeating a prayer with every bead of a rosary is an example of using a mantra. This practice helps induce a spiritual state in the person praying.

"You can use either single words or longer phrases when chanting a mantra. Examples of single words are 'Amen,' 'Allah,' 'Om,' and 'Alleluia.'

"Phrases that can be said are 'Dear Father in Heaven,' 'Hail Mary, Mother of God,' and 'Gloria in excelsis Deo,' which is a Christian mantra using Latin words. It means 'Glory to God in the highest.' 'Om Mani Padme Hum' is a Buddhist mantra that asks for compassion. A common Islamic saying is 'La elaha ill Allah hu,' which means 'There is no God except Allah.'

"A mantra helps you meditate because it keeps your attention focused. Your mind is less likely to wander and start thinking about ordinary concerns in your life. In addition, as you repeat your mantra, you continuously remind yourself to think of the meaning of the words, which guides you to harmonize with your spiritual Self.

"Many words, when said, sound like the meaning of the word. For example, the word 'clap' sounds similar to a clap of the hands. The same is true with the words 'hum' and 'yap.' If the words of a mantra sound like what the mantra is trying to induce, such as peace or love, its influence is greater.

"This is the case with Sanskrit, the language of ancient India. Sanskrit words vibrate with an energy that is equivalent to the meaning of each word.

"For example, the word 'shanti' means 'peace' in Sanskrit. It vibrates the same as the state of peace and tranquillity. 'Shanti' is pronounced with the accent on the first syllable. The letter 'a' sounds like 'ah' and the second syllable sounds like 'tea.'

 *Sanskrit symbol for "Om"*

"The same is true with the Sanskrit word 'Om.' Om represents God or the Divine. It stands for wholeness and unity, and is a common Hindu mantra. It can be said alone or used preceding other words or phrases. 'Om' is said with the mouth forming the 'o' sound and ending with the lips closed in 'm.' Chanting 'Om' brings about a calming and uplifting effect on your mind.

"Another way to say 'Om' is to pronounce it 'Aum.' The sound starts out with 'ow,' as in 'ouch.' It merges into the sound of 'oo,' as in 'oops.' It ends with the 'm' sound vibrating in your nasal region.

"Many words from other spiritual traditions trigger the same response as 'Om.' It happens when a Muslim says, 'Allah.' This means 'God' in the Islamic tradition. 'In the name of the Father, Son, and Holy Spirit,' from the Christian faith, means the same as 'Om.' The word 'Hu' is another word in the Islamic faith that means 'the presence of the Divine.'

"Christian words and phrases are recited in the same way a mantra is used. A commonly used word is 'Amen.' Said at the end of a prayer, it means 'It is so' or 'So be it.' 'Amen' originally came from Hebrew. Other prayers or Bible verses that are devotional in their effect are the Lord's Prayer and the Twenty-third Psalm.

"Mantras can be chanted silently or out loud. Repeating a mantra frequently during the day reminds you to think of your spiritual nature, which is peace and love. It can even help you manage stress."

At this time, I played for the class a wonderful tape of simple Hindu chants. I wrote out the words on my writing tablet so everyone could chant along with the tape.

Next, I led the class in reciting several other words and phrases used by different religious traditions, such as "Allah," "Alleluia," "Om shanti,"

"Amen," and "Aum."

After chanting as a group, I asked the members of the class to pick a mantra or prayer they particularly liked. I instructed them to close their eyes and quietly vocalize their mantra for awhile. I started by chanting the word "Om" and encouraged others to pick their own mantras. The room vibrated with a beautiful blend of different sounds.

After a few minutes, I asked the class members to spend some time meditating on the peace they experienced while saying their mantras. "If any of you finds your mind wandering, quietly repeat your mantra again."

When enough time had passed for the class members to complete their meditations, I asked, "So, what did you think about using a mantra?"

"I remember praying as a child and I felt the same way I did when I was young," Lisa shared.

"During our meditation, I particularly liked it when all of a sudden someone started chanting," Al stated. "It was very supportive in keeping me focused so my mind wouldn't wander."

"I didn't have the same kind of experience," Don said. "It's too bad, but I don't have a prayer that works for me. Thinking of church or praying reminds me of my childhood and how strict my father was. He used to force us to go to church. I don't have good memories about that."

"Maybe you can find a new way to pray which doesn't bring up your pain," Jane offered.

"I don't know," Don said. "It's pretty deep. I just try to forget about the past. You know, you have to move on."

As Anne was listening, she reflected on how past events continued to bother her. She liked Don's attitude about trying to forget about it all and moving on. She wondered what he did when old memories came back up in his mind. His comments gave her encouragement to let go of her resentments.

"Since it's late, let's adjourn. Try using different mantras along with your meditation this next week," I concluded.

NOTES

1. Awo Fa'lokun Fatunmbi, *Iba'se Orisa* (New York: Original Publications, 1994), p. 24.
2. Ibid., p. 23.

The Problems of the Personal Self

LEVELS OF CONSCIOUSNESS

Personal Self	Physical Body and Body Mind
	Emotional Body
	Lower Mental Body — *This is the everyday mind.*
Spiritual Self	Higher Mental Body — *This is the part of the mind that receives intuition and utilizes reason and wisdom.*
	Intuitional Body
	Field of Unity

"In this session, I will be concentrating on the personal self and how easy it is to get so wrapped up in it that you cut yourself off from the influence of your spiritual Self.

"Each aspect of the personal self — the body mind, the emotions, and the lower mental body — exerts a unique hold on your attention which prevents you from being open to the spiritual part of yourself.

"First of all, it is useful to review why the personal self exists at all. As

I said earlier, the manifestation of your spiritual Self on the physical plane has to have a strong instinct of self-preservation to insure its survival. This is the only way you can exist in a body.

"You can see this clearly in animals. Their instincts to avoid predators show up in their coloring, their mannerisms, and their reflexes. If you think about the creative way a bird feigns a broken wing or the speed with which a gazelle can jump up and run away if it is frightened, you can see the strength of the survival instinct.

"In a human being, the survival instinct is powerful, too. It takes the form of self-centeredness. You can say it is a form of self-love. The universal love of the spiritual Self, when operating within the personal self, insures self-preservation this way.

"This is a natural process in order to survive. On the physical level, the awareness of unity, which pervades everything, is not yet realized. Your consciousness is focused on taking care of your needs and your immediate concerns, such as your family.

"You are still the developing 'butterfly' within the cocoon of selfishness. Your consciousness can only discover and maintain an awareness of its true spiritual nature through many experiences over many lifetimes. It cannot happen all at once."

Al spoke up with a question. "I want to see if I understand you correctly when you say that consciousness becomes focused in the personal self. Let me take myself as an example. If I am focused in my personal self, then my awareness is only on myself and my own feelings. I don't think of anyone else. I react from my own point of view. Is that what you mean?"

I nodded, and Al continued. "Let me take it a bit further. If I stop reacting and think of how the other person must be feeling, then is my consciousness centered within my spiritual Self? It seems there is a quite a different point of view from that perspective."

"Very good, Al," I said. "That is the gist of what I am trying to teach. I would change the wording a bit and say your consciousness is *open* to the influence of your spiritual Self when you think of how another person must be feeling. To have your consciousness totally centered within your spiritual Self would be quite an accomplishment. The person would be Self-realized and able to remain in that state. An example of this type of person is Jesus or Buddha.

"I make this distinction because at our level of functioning we can utilize the influence of the spiritual Self, but we have not yet learned how to maintain it all the time. This takes a lot of practice and patience, most likely extending over many lifetimes.

"Because we're still learning, one moment we may be interacting with an openness to our intuition, and in the next moment, be thinking again only about what we want."

"Why is there so much variability?" asked Jane. "It seems so counter-productive."

"This is due to the nature of the spirit living on the physical plane," I said. "Because it lives in a body, it has an inborn self-interest. It can exist in no other way. This applies to emotional survival as well as physical survival. I will be focusing on your emotions in today's talk."

"Is there a way to be open to the influence of the spiritual Self, and at the same time be concerned about ourselves as well?" inquired Lisa.

"Good question," I said. "I believe there is. It is probably best said by using the word 'representing,' rather than 'concerned' about ourselves. This is the whole point of life. We need to be able to take care of ourselves, but at the same time look at the world and everything in it from the point of view of the spiritual Self with its realization of Unity. Understanding this and learning how to develop it is the goal of this class.

"When you interact in the world, whether at home or at work, you are using your personal self. You are thinking your everyday thoughts and going about the business of life. You may have moments of inspiration or deep understanding from your spiritual Self, but most of the time you are centered in your personal self. The moments of connection to your spiritual Self may be just brief flashes."

"What prevents these flashes from happening more often?" Al asked.

"The nature of the everyday mind prevents it," I answered. "When your mind is focused on day-to-day concerns, your thoughts are centered there. This changes when you pause and notice how much you love someone or take in the beauty of a sunset. At those times, you detach from what was occupying you so intently. Your mind becomes quiet. This allows you to have a wider focus and perceive things that are spiritual, as well as physical. You realize the Oneness of all.

"This usually doesn't last, however. Soon you find yourself once again wrapped up in the world of your personal self.

"Living in a physical body causes you to be subtly but perpetually influenced by a concern about yourself. One reason this happens is that the body mind is focused primarily on your survival. It relies on you and only you to keep your body healthy. Therefore, it must exert a strong influence so you don't get distracted and forget to do such necessary things as eat and sleep.

"In addition to your body mind, your emotional body will also sway you to think of yourself. It will come up with all sorts of desires which it thinks will make you happy. This, too, is only natural. It is simply doing its job. It influences you through your emotions to take care of yourself.

"In turn, this instinctive self-interest is evident in your everyday mind. It easily picks up on how you feel both physically and emotionally. It fills your mind with thoughts about yourself and what you want. Even when you think about your responsibilities, such as taking care of your children or going to work, you still have the underlying current of self-interest exerting a steady influence on your plans and decisions.

"There is nothing wrong with any of this. These preoccupations are necessary. They ensure the survival of the human species. The important thing is to be aware of it so you can make decisions utilizing your intelligence and your higher mind, rather than simply react to situations from your personal self with its built-in self-regard.

"It is hard to remember to do this when you are alone. This is when it is easiest to open to your spiritual Self. It is even harder to detach from your personal self when you are interacting with others. Your consciousness gets caught up in what is going on and you automatically operate from the point of view of your personal self.

"In relationships where it is easy to get along with the other person, the tendency for your consciousness to remain focused in your personal self is less strong. You can detach more frequently from its hold and display the qualities of your spiritual Self, such as unselfishness and love.

"In other relationships where a sense of mutual trust and rapport has broken down, it is more likely that conflicts will occur. The personal self acts on auto-pilot to protect itself. It perceives a threat to its sense of personal integrity and activates your defenses, which show up in a variety of ways."

DEFENSIVENESS

"I'm sure you all have encountered this. It is a common human experience. But reacting with any kind of defensiveness usually gets in the way of effective communication with others. It cuts you off from your ability to reason. You might feel like you can't think straight.

"Defensiveness is demonstrated in many ways. It can range from silence to arguing. It can show up through pouting, rebelling, being a martyr, walking away in a huff, withdrawing your love, or becoming depressed. They are unique to each person. There are as many ways as there are people."

"What determines how you get defensive?" Lisa asked.

"The manner in which defensiveness is demonstrated is influenced by your personality and how you have been conditioned to react," I said. "There are factors in your personality that are inherent, or inborn, as well as learned from your environment.

"One way you learn to respond to situations is from your parents' example. Parents are powerful teachers for children, who grow up and behave in similar ways.

"For example, if your mother or father yelled when under stress, it is likely that you learned to yell as well. If your family was quiet and dealt with difficult issues without discussion, you most likely learned to internalize your feelings and keep them to yourself."

"Isn't the personality also strongly influenced by the values of the culture in which you live?" inquired Al.

"Yes," I said. "For example, you learn the ways feelings are supposed to be expressed, as well as what is considered appropriate behavior for men and women."

"Can you inherit personality characteristics?" Jim asked.

"Yes, each of us has a genetic predisposition to certain personality traits," I said. "This shows up as early as infancy. When mothers reflect on their children's personalities as babies, they can see a correlation with how they act when they're older."

"I read an article summarizing the research on identical twins raised separately due to adoption," Al remarked. "It made the same point. There was a high incidence of similarities in the personalities of each set of twins. The studies concluded that the likenesses were caused by genetic factors. As you probably know, identical twins have the same set of genes. Personally, when I see the same characteristics in myself that were in my father, it is obvious where they came from."

"Good point, Al," I said. "The personality traits that a child has inherited will easily become manifested if the parents also display those qualities. This is the effect of modeling. For example, if a mother withdraws to her room when she is depressed, the child with the same tendency toward depression will probably learn to withdraw in a similar fashion.

"One reason your personality develops quirks and other ineffective reactions is the ease with which your body mind can be programmed. It can be trained to react in specific, habitual ways.

"If you recall from the discussion of the body mind in the first class, it can have 'a mind of its own.' Its reactions to events in your life are like reflexes over which you don't seem to have much control.

"In addition, because the body mind is the center of control for your survival instinct, it easily sparks defensive reactions. These can become routine. In turn, they trigger emotions of discomfort and dislike."

Don asked, "Is that why I find myself acting gruff and irritable for no apparent reason?"

"Probably. The body mind responds very rapidly. You often don't have a chance to think about how you are reacting. Most likely, you wouldn't choose to act that way if you had time to consider a different course of action. The body mind quickly arouses a variety of protective mechanisms.

"One situation where this is demonstrated is when you don't want to hear something that you perceive as negative. For example, if an authority figure, such as a teacher or a parent, corrects you on something, there can be an internal reaction of 'Not me. I don't do that.' But if the person speaks in a general way and refers to someone else when making a correction, you are more likely to listen openly to the information and see if it applies to you."

"Is fear involved with defensiveness?" Lisa asked. "It seems that this would be the reason the survival instinct gets activated."

FEAR

"Yes, you're exactly right," I said. "Underlying any defensive reaction is the feeling of fear. It puts the body mind on guard and readies you to ward off an attack or flee from a situation that may be unsafe.

"In most cases, however, when you get defensive, you are not actually physically threatened. You may be interacting with someone who is critical and you fear being degraded or embarrassed.

"Your physical reaction of tight muscles in your solar plexus may still occur, though, because your body mind doesn't know the difference. Then your consciousness gets drawn into your defenses. It is only natural for this to happen.

"The problem here is that you are unable to open to the influence of your higher mind and your spiritual Self. Your ability to reason is reduced. It can feel like you have a mental block and that you are being controlled by your emotions.

"Fear is the basis of most negative feelings and reactions. Situations may arise that cause you to feel disagreeable or irritated. If you look closely at why you feel this way, you will usually discover the element of fear.

"For example, you may fear being exposed in some way that will cause you to be ashamed of yourself, or you may fear feeling guilty about something. If you have been humiliated, you fear being shown to be inadequate. In addition, you may be afraid if you defended yourself, you would be subjected to additional abuse."

"I had a terrible time accepting the death of my mother," Jane said. "How does this relate to fear?"

"Difficulty with grief after a loving parent's death may be caused by the fear that you will never get over the loss, or the fear you won't be loved in the same way again," I answered.

"I never thought of it like this before," Jane said, "but I was afraid I would never feel good again. My mother and I were very close. That is what I miss. I guess I had fears about what would happen to me when my mother's love was gone."

"This is very common," I said. "Let's examine it a bit. Underlying fear of all kinds is a more basic fear that something is wrong with you. It is a fear of being found to be unsatisfactory or lacking in some way. It implies that, at a fundamental level, you are undeserving of acceptance and love.

"Taking this one step further, if you feel unlovable, it implies you are unworthy of life itself. This triggers an even more basic fear. That is the fear of death. It is usually experienced unconsciously, which means you are not aware of it.

"But if you explore your feelings deeply, feeling unacceptable poses a threat to your basic sense of survival. It implies you don't have a right to exist. This kind of doubt activates the survival instinct to set up a defense against it. It will try to ward off anything that seems threatening. It is a mechanism built into the body mind to protect the vehicle of expression of your spiritual Self."

"Are there other ways a person can handle these fears?" Lisa asked.

"Yes," I said. "One way the personal self counteracts the fear of being unlovable is through the desire to be special. When you are growing up, if you feel special, you are reassured that you are loved and accepted. Not only does this feel good emotionally, but at a deep level it also helps you feel your survival is guaranteed. You are reassured that you won't be forgotten when it comes to being fed or given the necessities of life.

"The desire to be special is what motivates sibling rivalry. There is competition between brothers and sisters for attention and approval from their parents.

"All of this is done unconsciously. You do not decide with your conscious mind to look for love and approval. It happens automatically."

"Is this desire satisfied when men and women fall in love and marry?" Jane asked.

"Yes, the most common way people satisfy the yearning to be special is through a love relationship, such as marriage," I said. "It provides a sense of security through commitment and loving support. Because men and women are complementary, they feel more complete through this kind of bond. Their love is an expression of the unity of the spiritual Self.

"Your mind also plays an active part in the desire to feel special. Because the purpose of the mental body is to judge and discriminate, you ascertain how you stand in comparison with others. You judge yourself and others to decide if you are better or fall short. Naturally, you want to find that your qualities are acceptable."

"Is this why people spend so much time in front of the mirror trying to look good?" Al asked.

"Or get consumed with finding the right mate?" Lisa added.

"Yes, these are all manifestations of the same basic drive," I responded.

"Such behaviors aren't necessary, however. If you become aware of the reasons why people yearn to feel special, you realize that everyone is special in his or her own unique way. You are all a part of a greater unity that pervades everything.

"I am reminded about an educational television program from the 1980s that featured a woman who had terminal cancer. The topic of the program was the dying process. It focused on the woman's course of medical treatment and her death several months later. It was a good program on the process of death and dying.

"One conversation the woman had with the interviewer still stands out in my mind. She was sharing her feelings about having a terminal illness. She said that, throughout her illness, she had an unwavering belief that she was special and wouldn't really succumb to her cancer. She felt other people would normally die from her disease, but that she would be an exception.

"This demonstrates an important point. When the woman said she always believed she would survive her cancer, there was a part of her that knew this was true. This was her spiritual Self, which never dies.

"The problem arose because she was looking at the situation from the point of view of her personal self. She misinterpreted what her intuition knew to be true and thought it would be her physical body that would survive her illness. This shows how easy it is to identify with your personal self and think it is all you are.

"Since fear is the underlying motivation for so many things you do in life, I'd like to lead you through a class exercise about it. Fear is most likely not in your conscious awareness. Because of this, let me ask you some questions that will help uncover its influence on you."

I asked everyone to write down all the fears they were aware of. "You may have a fear of your husband or wife dying, or of something happening to your children. You may fear losing your job or your health. List all the fears you can think of."

After a few minutes, I explained I would be starting some sentences and leaving the endings blank for the class to fill in. Whatever came to each person's mind was to be written down on the paper.

" 'The worst part of losing my job would be. . . .'

"Reflect on how this would be for you. What is your catastrophic expectation associated with losing your job?

" 'The worst part about losing my spouse, or loved one, would be. . . .'

"What would be the catastrophe you would experience if your spouse died?"

I read a number of other sentences for the class to finish, such as:

The worst part about losing my eyesight would be . . . .

. . . my thinking ability . . . .

. . . my looks. . . .

. . . my health. . . .

. . . my parents. . . .

. . . my ability to walk. . . .

. . . my children. . . .

We discussed the exercise and found a common fear people had was some sort of basic threat to their physical integrity or survival. This involved the fear of losing one's home, job, or the ability to care for oneself.

"What about anger? Is fear involved with anger?" Don asked.

ANGER

"Yes, fear is the common root, even under angry feelings," I said. "Anger is considered to be a secondary reaction, with more basic feelings as your primary emotions, such as humiliation, shame, or hurt. Anger is an instinctive reaction designed to protect you. It works to oppose the person or situation that initially caused your pain. Anger also releases the energy that builds up when you feel wronged.

"Let's look at an example which shows how fear is mixed into anger. If your car gets rear-ended, you may get mad. Along with your anger, you probably have several fears. You may be afraid of your spouse's reaction to the accident. You may fear you will have problems getting to your job because your car is wrecked. It may trigger fears about how much it will cost to get your car fixed.

"You can be legitimately exasperated at the person who drove his car into yours. However, if you don't have fear involved under your frustration, you can remain somewhat detached about the situation, rather than become enraged.

"Sometimes fear prompts you to suppress your anger, which results in other problems. As I mentioned earlier, curbing your anger may cause you to internalize your feelings, which can lead to depression. You may direct your anger at yourself, resulting in guilt or low self-esteem. It can also cause buried resentment because you don't have a chance to resolve whatever it was that brought about your anger in the first place."

"Is there a purpose to anger?" Al queried. "It seems there is a purpose for everything that exists in life. How does anger fit into the whole scheme of things?"

"Anger serves the purpose of telling you something is wrong," I explained. "If a situation comes up that you don't like, your body mind signals this to you through physical cues, such as tense muscles in your solar plexus. This is where the expression 'getting uptight' comes from. In turn, your emotional body experiences dissatisfaction and discomfort. You don't feel good. This calls the mind into play, which recognizes something isn't right and probably needs to be changed.

"It has been said that feeling anger is useful for only a fraction of a second. This means you experience it just long enough to receive the signal that something is wrong, but not so you vent it on anyone.

"Expressing anger to others isn't the goal. Rather, the goal is for you to evaluate the cause of your anger. You need to assess the situation and decide what is necessary to be done to take care of yourself or others.

"When you vent anger on someone, it usually accompanies the release of muscular tension built up by your body mind in its protective stance. Releasing this is why people say they feel better after they have gotten mad. This isn't a good way to get rid of your tensions, but it helps explain why it happens.

"An expression I heard from my grandmother warns of the results of discharging anger: 'When you burn with the fire of anger, smoke gets in your eyes.' The 'smoke' in your eyes clouds your vision so you can't see the effect you are having on others. You become consumed by your anger and may take it out on someone else. Your objective thinking is blocked. That's why she would say that anger is only one letter short of 'danger.'

"This is also expressed in the Yoruba religion by the saying, 'When water boils over the side of the pot, it smothers the flame.'[1] The boiling water is your anger, which smothers the flame of your spiritual Self.

"Expressing anger in certain ways can become a habit. Let us look at an example. If a mother is in a hurry to get to work and her children are dawdling, she may get angry and yell at them. Her stress results from the fear that she will be late for work. This connects to a deeper fear she may lose her job and then not have income to support herself and her children.

"All of this creates tension. When she meets an obstacle, such as her children refusing to get dressed, she is unable to suppress her frustrations and gets mad at them. She vents her feelings and uses the power of her anger to get them to cooperate. The mother may even recognize she is in a repetitive cycle of tension and release, but feel powerless to stop herself."

"How does this mother learn to change her behavior?" Jane asked.

"Change must happen at several levels," I said. "It is referred to as 'the ABCs of change.' This means in order for change to happen, it must affect several areas within you. They are the affective, the behavioral, and the cognitive.

"The 'A,' or the affective, is the emotional part of yourself. You must deal with your *feelings* about the issue in order to change. In the example of the mother who yells at her children, she must look at all her feelings, even her fears, and any others that are unresolved within her.

"The 'B,' or the behavioral, means you must work on changing your *behavior* in order to fully alter your habits. For example, you can employ anger control techniques to prevent losing your temper.

"The 'C,' or the cognitive, represents your mind. In order to change, you must develop your thinking to gain insight about the meaning of your problems. You must *understand* not only why you act the way you do and what triggers your reactions, but also the various steps you must go through to change your behavior for the better.

"In the example of the mother who gets angry at her children for making her late for work, finding a solution about how time can better be used in the morning is an example of using the cognitive level to solve a problem.

"In order to successfully change, all three components — the affective, the behavioral, and the cognitive — need to be worked on.

"By the way, the 'ABCs' also reflect the three levels of the personal self. The affective component is the emotional body. The behavioral component is the physical body and body mind. The cognitive element is the mental body. As you strengthen your understanding of how these elements work together, you can employ all three levels in the process of change and gain more control over your personal self.

"There is a saying that supports the process of changing negative expressions of anger: 'Anger makes the knife tempered to a more perfect edge.' The 'knife' can be used to 'cut' up whomever you are mad at, or it can be used to 'cut' through your own conflicting emotions and urges to understand what is underneath. Then you can see how you feel and what you need to do about it. Ultimately, anger is a tool for growth. Working to overcome it strengthens you.

"There is something else to keep in mind about change. It is important to realize that successful change usually happens from 'backwards to forwards.' This means you normally can't change negative reactions simply by making a commitment never to repeat them again. Accomplishing it this way is rare.

"Take the example of getting irritated at someone. What normally happens is the unwanted behavior comes up in yourself again, even if you have made a strong commitment to rid yourself of it. Changing it must be done in stages.

"At first, the important thing to do is be aware of yourself becoming impatient and irritated. Usually, you won't be able to stop it. When you see yourself this way, affirm — either silently or out loud — that you want to change. Watch your reactions and make every effort to curtail yourself. Gradually, you will be able to stop yourself sooner and sooner after you have become mad.

"Even though you may repeat your unwanted behavior, don't give up. Once you have stopped yourself, even if it is in the middle of an unpleasant interchange, force yourself to act the way you want to act.

"You won't necessarily feel this way throughout. This is the stage where you 'fake it until you make it.' With practice, you will learn to curb your irritability so you will only be tempted to show it. Eventually, you will find yourself displaying calmness and understanding even under stress.

"In some cases, it may be necessary to seek the help of an anger management counselor, particularly if anger is displayed frequently and abusively. Harmful expressions of anger must be stopped in any way possible because of the detrimental effects on the family.

"There is an expression that refers to the habitual ways anger gets triggered. It is called 'button-pushing.' When someone pushes your button, he does something that will likely elicit an angry response from you.

"An example of 'button-pushing' is the teenager who leaves her room a mess. This pushes the button of the mother, who gets angry and can't compromise about it, because the messy room holds a deeper meaning for her. The mother fears if her house is a mess, she will be judged as incompetent. She may also feel, at an underlying level, her daughter doesn't care enough about her if she lets her room get messy. From the point of view of the mother's body mind, if her daughter really cared, she wouldn't do something to put her mother at risk of being judged.

"There is also an underlying meaning in the messy room for the daughter. It represents independence and freedom from her parents' control. The daughter needs to make her own way in life and develop self-confidence. She needs to know she can take care of herself, instead of remaining dependent on her family. The messy room symbolically starts the breaking-away process from the safety of her parents' home.

"Each person has his or her own individual set of 'buttons.' They are all formed in a unique way, because no two people or the circumstances in which they live are the same. You have to explore the meaning of your own buttons to understand them."

"You said that fear is the basis of most negative feelings," Al said. "What about jealousy or envy? Is fear tied in with them?"

"Yes, jealousy is the fear of being replaced," I said. "If you are jealous of someone, you fear they are better than you. At an underlying level, you worry you will be rejected and replaced by the person you feel is superior.

"Envy has its basis in the fear you cannot create what someone else has done. Again, it relates to the fear of inadequacy. You fear that you are unacceptable at a fundamental level if you cannot match what someone else has accomplished.

"Fear is underneath other feelings, such as greed and arrogance. Greed is the fear of not having enough of something. Arrogance results from the fear you don't know enough. All these reactions are related to feelings of inadequacy.

"You have probably heard of the expression, 'You have nothing to fear, but fear itself.' This comes from Franklin D. Roosevelt's first inaugural address. The same idea has also been stated in the Bible, in Proverbs 3:25, and by other writers, such as Montaigne and Thoreau.

"Fear has been called 'the enemy within.' This is your self-doubt. It is far greater in its effect on you than anything you can be afraid of outside yourself."

WORRY

"Worry is also the result of fear. Worry is repeatedly thinking of something you are apprehensive or concerned about. When you worry, your thoughts create energy. This energy makes a thought-form that remains in your environment. It influences you to rethink the same thought. If you spend time mulling it over when it pops back into your mind, you add more energy to it. This keeps the process going. Only by thinking about something totally different can you interrupt this cycle.

"There is an important principle in the Polynesian/Hawaiian tradition called 'makia,'[2] which means 'energy flows where your attention goes.' Wherever you direct your attention, energy will flow to it. For example, if you worry about something, each time it comes up in your mind, energy flows into it, which only makes it more likely to occur to you once again.

"You can find this happening with any emotion. If you think of things that make you angry, you increase your resentment every time you go over them in your mind."

"What should we do if we are worried about someone?" Anne asked.

"This is an important question because most people worry at one time or another. If I told you never to worry again, it would be pointless. You wouldn't be able to stop yourself.

"Worry comes up naturally in your mind. What you can do to change it is learn to be aware of it when it first occurs. Then you can interrupt the process. Usually, worry involves a sense of dread — there is something you don't want to happen. The best thing to do when you get worried is to think of its opposite. You can counteract the negative energy of worry by picturing something positive.

"For example, if you are worried about an upcoming presentation you have to make at work, don't let yourself think about stumbling over your words or appearing incompetent. Think of presenting your speech with poise and confidence. Picture yourself acting self-assured and capable.

"Taking this example a little further, you may recognize that you are specifically worried about not knowing an answer to a question. What you can do for this is to envision yourself calmly responding with something like, 'I don't know, but I will find out.'

"There are many negative feelings, in addition to worry, that you can modify in yourself by thinking of their positive counterparts. Hippocrates, the Greek physician, spoke of this when he said, 'Opposites are cures for opposites.' "

Jim said, "I was in a seminar which taught that you should do something physical if you are stuck in a repetitive pattern of worry. Because worry consumes your mind, physically doing something different can take you out of that process. They suggested taking a bicycle ride or working in your garden."

"It works, too," Al said. "Sometimes when I am troubled by something at the office, I will go to my Bible study class. Then I'm able to come home refreshed and free of those worries. Changing your circumstances really can make a difference."

"What can I do when I worry about my children?" asked Anne.

"This is common for parents," I said. "It is understandable for you to worry about loved ones if they do something out of the ordinary, such as take a trip. What you can do is to send them love.

"Imagine them surrounded by light. Think of the light as an energy that will insure their safety. Remember, if you think of them with worry, that energy goes to them. This is the opposite feeling you want to transmit. Being aware of this is a motivation for you to consciously change your thinking."

Don expressed doubt. "It seems hard to believe that what I think will affect someone who is far away from me."

"Your skepticism is important," I told him. "Remember not to believe anything someone says unless is rings true within you.

"I'll try to explain some of the factors in a case like this. Certainly, the power of thought has limits. If you send loving energy to someone who is engaged in a risky behavior, your energy may offer little help. Your thoughts may have only a subtle influence. However, you may be able to reinforce that person's own sensible thinking, should it arise within him.

"What do the rest of you think about this?" I asked the class.

Al said he knew a woman who could signal her husband when he was at work that she wanted him to call her by mentally picturing him picking up the telephone and dialing their phone number. Pretty soon, her phone would be ringing with her husband on the other end.

Jane said, "Have you ever entered a room of people and picked up a sense about what was going on? I usually can feel the vibes in a room."

A couple of people said they had had experiences similar to Jane's.

"I haven't experienced anything like this," Don said.

"It's okay if you haven't picked up on the thoughts and feelings of others," I said. "It isn't necessarily a thing to be desired. The people who are particularly sensitive find it troublesome at times. They can be like a sponge, picking up negative as well as positive energy."

Jane said she had experienced feeling wiped out by the impact of a tense situation. She described how she felt drained of her energy and physically tired and stiff. She wondered if there was anything she could do about it.

"I have heard advice about this subject," I told her. "The speaker described how you could put up an imaginary shield around yourself to ward off negative energy from others. However, she said the shield would also prevent you from dissipating the energy from your own negative feelings and thoughts. It would remain clustered around you.

"Because I am not experienced in this type of thing, I would recommend something else. One way to protect yourself is to think about the unity of all. This helps you rise above the level of your personal self and feel a sense of acceptance and universal love.

"Emanating love and understanding prevents you from picking up other people's negativity. This is a state of being centered within your spiritual Self.

"What can you do about negative feelings that come up in yourself?" Lisa asked.

"That's exactly what I was going to talk about next," I said. "First of all, I would like us to do a brainstorming exercise about the ways you can counteract negative thinking. Call out to me all the negative feelings you can think of and I'll record them on my writing easel."

Quite a long list was made. "Now, I'd like you to think of a positive feeling that would counteract each of these negative emotions. For example, if you feel jealous of someone, you can work against that negativity by feeling happy for the person you are jealous of. Another example is irritability. You can work on being patient to counteract it."

As the class discussed each negative emotion, there was some disagreement over what would be the best feeling to nurture if you experienced anger. Some people said it would be best to feel accepting of the other person. Others said calmness would be the best antidote for anger.

Another stimulating discussion came up over argumentativeness. It was thought being silent would be the way to counteract the urge to argue. Others felt welcoming someone else's point of view would be the feeling to adopt.

The highlights of the list were:

COUNTERACTING NEGATIVE FEELINGS

	Negative Feeling		Its Opposite
To overcome:	impatience	work on feeling:	calmness
	resentment		forgiveness
	harshness		kindness
	possessiveness		generosity
	animosity		thinking of the other's good qualities
	selfishness		unselfishness
	vanity		humility
	criticism		compliments
	arrogance		humility
	suspicion		trust
	indifference		compassion
	insecurity		confidence
	hate		love

"What if you get frustrated with someone and you realize it was really his issue that came up between you?" Jim asked.

"Are you referring to someone who entangles you in his problems and takes out his anger on you?" I said.

"Yes," Jim replied.

"First of all, you can be assured every time you get exasperated or mad, you are reacting that way because *your* issues are being triggered. Another person may draw you into his problems, but your reactions are your responsibility.

"Your issues are getting sparked, such as impatience, defensiveness, or fear. When you remain neutral to other people's anger or emotions, then you can see the issue only comes from them.

"Sometimes you can get drawn into someone else's stresses. He or she may take out frustrations on you by being irritable. When this happens, step back from the situation. Do not react. Watch what the other person is doing and notice your feelings. You will have more clarity about what is going on. You may be able to trace an argument back to its source and notice if you got drawn into something, or if you share responsibility for the start of the trouble."

BLAME

"If someone else acts in a way that causes you to become angry, resist the tendency to blame them for your behavior," I said. "You are still the one responsible for how you react.

"Blaming someone else relieves you of the burden of guilt for your actions. It is based in fear and isn't necessary. It is an avoidance behavior designed to protect yourself.

"Instead of blaming another, look at why you feel the way you do. If you plant flowers and they don't blossom, you don't blame the flowers. You find out why they didn't bloom. The same idea applies to yourself. Work on your own issues rather than try to change someone else. The following saying makes this point: 'When you master yourself, you don't need to master others.'

"Aristophanes, one of the classical Greek poets and writers, warned of the folly of trying to change another person when he wrote, 'You cannot teach a crab to walk straight.' This saying points out that you need to accept other people as they are.

"Criticizing others protects you from self-criticism. When you find fault in another, you can focus elsewhere and not look at yourself. You can avoid feeling guilty or ashamed.

"Usually, the faults you see in another are in yourself, as well. That is why you can see them so well. You are familiar with them. You just don't want to consider them a part of you.

"There is a Native American expression that warns you of this: 'Never point your finger at someone outside your circle because you have three fingers pointing back at yourself.'[3]

I demonstrated this by holding up my arm with my hand out in front. I pointed my index finger straight ahead. The other fingers were closed against my palm, in effect pointing back at me.

"This graphically depicts how criticizing someone else means you must first work on yourself to correct your own personality faults. Confucius said, 'When you see a man of worth, think of how you may emulate him. When you see one who is unworthy, examine your own character.' This means that when you find someone you think is unworthy, you must examine yourself to see why you feel that way. Discover if you have the same qualities or why you feel it necessary to judge them and feel superior.

"The part of your personality you don't like and don't want to face is your 'shadow side.' These are qualities in yourself you don't want to accept. If you keep your undesirable characteristics in the 'shadow,' or out of your awareness, you can live under the illusion that you are free from them.

"This is all part of the defensive nature of the protective lower self. It narrows your thinking so you can't see what you are doing. Analyzing this can help you overcome it."

PROJECTION

"Another problem that comes up in relationships is projection. Projection happens when you 'project,' or conclude another person is feeling or acting a particular way about you because of your own worries and fears. For example, if you are concerned that other people will try to dominate or control you, you are more likely to jump to the conclusion that this is happening. It may or may not be true in reality, but that doesn't matter. You are convinced that your conclusion is correct, and you react on that basis.

"Let us look at another example to see how projection comes about. Imagine a little boy whose parents expect a lot of him. He feels pressure to do well and interprets his parents' corrections as disapproval of who he is. He worries whether he will ever measure up.

"In adulthood, he gets married. Because of his conditioning, he expects he won't receive his wife's approval either. In reality, she may not be disapproving at all. This doesn't make any difference, however, because the man has learned to expect disapproval from those close to him. It is what he felt with his parents, and he automatically anticipates it from others.

"This process is called 'projection.' The man projects onto his wife that she is being critical. He then reacts like it really happened and feels inadequate. He may also get mad at her, something he couldn't do in his childhood out of fear of his parents.

"Projection is something you learn to do through conditioning. It is like a bad habit. The only way to overcome it is through the insight of your higher mind, which allows you to see when you are getting defensive because of your own misinterpretation.

"Another example of projection is a woman who as a child didn't receive love and approval from her father. She marries a man who is powerful like her father was. She worries about her faults and fears he will stop loving her. She feels she doesn't live up to his standards and is afraid he will leave her.

"Those very fears make the relationship less rewarding for the husband, who might become dissatisfied with the marriage as a result. This only confirms to the woman that she was right all along. It all stems from the belief she took on as a child that she is unlovable.

"Since this is very complex, sorting it out may require the help of a therapist. This can be very beneficial. Not only can you find relief from negative patterns in your relationships, but you can also resolve painful childhood memories.

"People tend to choose partners who will recreate a family structure similar to the one they grew up in. This is not only from familiarity, but also from learned patterns of interaction developed in childhood.

"You probably have heard it said that a girl marries a man similar to her father and a boy marries a woman who is like his mother. This is not done consciously. When you marry, it may not seem like there are similarities to your opposite-sexed parent. But because of what you learned as a child, you expect the same kind of interactions you had with your parents.

"This pattern of repetition can be broken by being aware of it as it happens. You can decide to make the changes your parents never implemented. Watching yourself can help you prevent having problems similar to the ones in the family you grew up in.

"To a certain extent, all families are dysfunctional. There are no perfect people in the world. Subsequently, there are no perfect families in which to grow up. You can learn from the faults of your parents and improve yourself in the process. Then you can work to prevent passing the same patterns on to your own children.

"Everything you encounter in life provides an opportunity for growth and learning. The struggles of your childhood, your parents' imperfections, and your own personality quirks all provide the necessary conditions for your evolution. They all contribute to your becoming a perfect expression of your spiritual Self.

"If you think about the multitude of wonderful qualities in your spiritual Self, there must be a multitude of experiences in your life for you to develop and perfect those qualities. They all make a contribution.

"When any negative trait is overcome, your spiritual Self shines through and manifests itself on the physical plane. This can happen only through experience. From overcoming the bad, the positive is born.

"Developing your awareness about all of this is the purpose of life. When you become conscious of a negative trait and make efforts to overcome it, the result is like a rose among thorns. The rose is an expression of your spiritual Self. The thorns are those negative traits and qualities that you have yet to confront. It is said the best rose bush is not the one with the fewest thorns, but the one that bears the finest roses. Thorns are a part of life. You cannot be perfect from the beginning.

"You learn by doing. With every mistake, you grow. The poet Robert Frost said, 'The only way out is through.' This refers to the struggle you have to go through to resolve anything. You must face it straight on. It is the process which allows you to learn.

"Zen Buddhism has a metaphor that pertains to the same principle. It says, 'The coin lost in the mud must be retrieved from the mud.' This means you need to go through both the highs and lows of life in order develop yourself. The 'coin' refers to your spiritual Self obscured by your personal self in the 'mud' of day-to-day life. Getting down in the mud is the only way you can retrieve the coin."

FORGIVENESS

"An important part of this growth process is forgiveness — forgiveness of others who have done things to hurt you as well as forgiveness of yourself. Because this is difficult to achieve, I'd like to lead you through a guided meditation that will help you in this direction. Please get into a comfortable position, close your eyes, and take a few cleansing breaths."

Don thought to himself that he didn't want to go through another meditation. He couldn't see that he benefited much from them. He also thought he didn't have much within himself he needed to forgive. He knew he had made his share of mistakes, but he felt people should accept him the way he was. Deep down, he felt others knew he was a good person. When the meditation started, he reluctantly took part.

Anne sensed she carried a lot of accumulated stress. She worried she would start to cry during the meditation. Nevertheless, she decided to try the exercise and not feel self-conscious.

"Let us feel harmony with the group," I began. "Picture yourself in a peaceful setting in nature. Feel the sun on your skin, hear the birds in the sky and the wind blowing through the trees. Experience the harmony that is a part of nature."

After a pause, I continued, "Think of someone you love and send love to them. Send love to your entire family.

"Open your heart and send love to the surrounding community.

"Shifting things in your mind, think of someone toward whom you feel anger. Picture this person standing about six feet in front of you. Recall the events that brought about your anger.

"Open your heart once again and realize the sense of wholeness and completeness within you.

"Look at the person and silently say, 'I forgive you for what you have done to me in the past.'

"Let the feeling of forgiveness expand in your heart. Say again, 'I forgive you.'

"Allow a sense of healing to develop inside yourself. It is from a position of health and wellness that you extend forgiveness to the other person.

"Send feelings of good will to the person.

"Imagine yourself feeling this way in the future.

"Now, slowly and gently, let that person fade from your awareness. Turn your attention to yourself. Recall things you have done in the past that you regret. Pay attention to the criticism you have for yourself.

"Allow a sense of self-forgiveness to come over you. Say the words silently, 'I forgive myself.'

"Realize your own inner goodness. Know deep in your heart that you are worthy of love and acceptance. Say again silently, 'I forgive myself.'

"Let yourself feel the kindness of forgiveness. Imagine feeling this way in the future as you make mistakes again. Know that you will learn from your errors and are deserving of understanding and compassion. Repeat the words, 'I forgive myself.'

"Fill your heart with love. Open your heart to encompass the whole world."

After a final pause, I concluded, "Taking the time you need, come back to the group and open your eyes.

"How was this experience for you?"

Lisa spoke first. "I was surprised at how much feeling I had inside about my father. He was the one I chose to forgive. He was pretty harsh with me as I grew up. As I pictured him standing in front of me, I saw him feeling guilty and actually wanting my forgiveness. I wouldn't say I have totally forgiven him, but this is a start. Frankly, I think I am still a little afraid of him."

"What is it with fathers that they can't be more caring?" Jane said, exasperated. "The person I had to forgive was my dad, too. His problems were around alcohol, though. So I guess I can't totally blame him, since alcoholism is now considered a disease."

"You both opened up some wounds within yourselves with this exercise," I said. "I'd like to make a suggestion. Because you are holding on to the same feelings you had when you were young children, you will benefit from doing this exercise again on your own. If you repeat this daily for a week or so, you will see a change within yourself. You will alter your internalized view of who you are and, in essence, 'grow up' in relation to your fathers. You will leave behind the position of a hurt and helpless child, because forgiveness comes from a position of confidence and power. You will 'grow' into a new self-image of assurance and strength."

"I see what you mean," Lisa acknowledged, "but I don't think I could ever feel I had equal power to my father."

Don spoke up, "You have to realize he was stuck with his own hang-ups and problems which didn't allow him to do any better. His dad probably raised him in the same way he treated you."

"I know men are conditioned to appear strong and in control," Jim offered. "When fathers have to deal with kids, however, things seem out of control. Unknowingly, we can get a little heavy-handed."

"Mothers can also get carried away with punishment as they raise their children," Jane interjected. "It isn't only fathers who can cause problems. I have some memories of the way I treated my children which I worked on during the meditation on self-forgiveness."

The class members continued to discuss the meditation exercise and their individual experiences. Anne was glad that she didn't have to say anything. She had held in her tears during the meditation, but felt that she would lose control if she started talking. She had so many disappointments from people in her past. She thought she had resolved them all but could see the need to work on more forgiveness.

Don said he got more out of the self-forgiveness portion of the meditation than he had from all the other meditations combined. He felt he needed to forgive himself because he came across as too brusque, particularly to his wife.

"It is important to develop an ease with self-forgiveness," I said. "Self-criticism is never useful. The point is to learn from your mistakes and work on ways to prevent them in the future. Be kind toward yourself. A little poem my grandmother gave me speaks to this:

> "When you have made an awful blunder,
> "Don't bewail your brainless act.
> "Think of all your past successes.
> "Give yourself a little tact.

"A client told me once that too much self-criticism or *analysis* can lead to *paralysis*. Then you need *dialysis* to get over it. I like that play on words. It emphasizes the point so well."

"That is exactly what happens to me," Lisa chimed in. "I am too hard on myself. Things keep coming up again and again in my mind. It is hard to let them go."

"That is common. But it is something you really need to watch because of the self-programming you can do to your body mind. Remember, it takes in information like a sponge. The things you say or think about yourself stay within you and form the basis of your self-image."

BELIEFS

"Your personal view of who you are is composed of a series of statements and beliefs about yourself. You may not realize the kinds of things you hold as beliefs, but they are there, subtly but steadily influencing you. Their power can be great, particularly the ones that limit you or hold you back.

"To point out the influence of a belief, let's look at a specific example. If you believe you are incapable of doing something, such as climbing a ladder, it will be difficult to do it when the time comes. Your body may shake and you might get dizzy or become 'paralyzed' at any point on the ladder. You may also have a 'pit' in your stomach from fear. If you had the belief you could learn to do almost anything, you might still have fear, but you would overcome it more easily."

"How are beliefs formed?" Lisa asked.

"Beliefs are formed as you go about your life," I answered. "First of all, you perceive your world through the senses of your physical body. This, in turn, stimulates your emotional body, which reacts to what you are experiencing. Your mind takes it all in and correlates it with what has happened in the past. It then comes to a decision about your experience.

"You decide if it was pleasurable and acceptable, or if it should be avoided. You draw conclusions and make generalizations, such as 'The world is a safe place,' 'The world is unfriendly,' 'Authority figures can (or cannot) be trusted,' 'Life is hard,' or 'Life is good.'

"Beliefs about who you are result from a variety of different kinds of input. You may have things said to you that shape how you feel about yourself. The ways people act toward you give you further information. For example, if you are treated poorly, you may conclude you don't deserve anything better. On the other hand, accomplishments and achievements contribute to a positive sense of self-worth.

"Experiences from your childhood and the way you were raised are major determinants of your self-esteem. If you received negative statements when you were growing up, you will probably hold on to those ideas and allow them to continue influencing you.

"Many times, however, you may draw faulty and inaccurate conclusions about yourself. If you keep quiet about them, no one will ever have a chance to set you straight.

"Take the example of a large family where one child develops severe health problems. The parents may be emotionally stressed worrying about his condition. Much of their time goes to taking care of the sick child. They may not be able to fully meet the emotional needs of their other children. Some of the children may be assertive enough to get attention. But a non-assertive child who doesn't actively seek out contact with his parents may grow up feeling he is unimportant and unworthy of love.

"This is a flawed conclusion made from a child's point of view. Because children have difficulty expressing what they think and feel, the parents may never find out about their child's mistaken belief and correct it.

"But the child takes it for granted and it becomes part of his identity. It may even act as a repelling force to any idea that contradicts it. For example, if the child receives a compliment, he may not believe it or point out what he thinks are his shortcomings.

"Your belief system can also be learned by imitating your parents. If one of your parents feels low self-esteem, you may copy this and adopt the same view for yourself. Other complex psychological patterns can also be learned through modeling. An example of this is depression.

"Sometimes problems can be traced back many generations. This doesn't have to be discouraging, however. Recognizing that a problem has its roots far back in your family tree can relieve you of the burden of guilt for having it. You can then learn more effective ways to deal with it so it doesn't continue as strongly into the next generation.

"Developing a healthy self-esteem doesn't come naturally. Even in the most ideal family circumstances, children still have problems feeling good about themselves. Upon reaching adulthood, most people have yet to develop a solid self-acceptance. It is considered an adult developmental task to acquire a healthy self-regard.

"When you have incorporated a negative belief system about your-self, it is made up of a group of thoughts. They may be 'I am stupid,' 'I am unattractive,' 'I am not worth much,' 'Nobody cares about me,' or 'I can't do it.' Each thought is composed of a collection of energy which makes up a thought-form.

"On the mental plane, the energy from negative thought-forms influences your thinking by blocking thoughts that contradict it. Your motivation to do things that go against it is also inhibited. It then stimulates emotions that accompany the negative thoughts, such as shame, guilt, or depression.

"Beliefs are not forgotten, even though you may forget about the specific circumstances that formed them in the first place. They settle into your body mind along with the fear and shame. They influence you to repeat the same patterns of behavior that both stem from and reinforce the beliefs.

"You become accustomed to these actions and their familiarity seems safe. This satisfies the body mind and its protective instinct. You can say the conditioned ways of interacting in the world are within your 'comfort zone.' This makes it hard for you to change and try anything new. You continue with your life in the same way as always. Some call this a 'rut,' like the rut a wagon wheel can get stuck in on a dirt road.

"Leaving your comfort zone to make changes in your life is difficult. There is a tendency to fall back into your habitual ways of behaving. There are many examples of this. If you leave a relationship that is uncaring, you may find yourself in another relationship with similar characteristics. You tend to choose a person whose treatment of you is familiar.

"Taking another example, in the workplace, you may limit yourself by staying in a job you are used to but find boring. You may doubt your qualifications for another job which would be more challenging and fulfilling.

"The reluctance to change your life is strong, but it can be overcome. When you make a change for the better, you are utilizing the guidance of your spiritual Self. This influence gives you the strength of will to stop repeating a negative pattern. Will is unlimited. It comes from your spiritual Self, which is unlimited in every way.

"If you find you need to make a change, trust yourself that you can do it. My grandmother used to tell me if my life seemed to run into a brick wall, it didn't mean I should give up. Instead, it meant I needed to make a turn to my 'right.' This, then, was the right path for me.

"Holding on to beliefs can block you from fulfilling your potential. They can prevent your from making positive changes in your life. Beliefs come from thoughts, which influence your attitudes, feelings, and ultimately your actions.

"Most people try to change actions rather than thoughts. Actions are actually harder to change. It is much easier to change how you think. This is where your power is. You are just three inches away from anything you want. This is the three inches to the inside of your brain.

"There is an expression that illustrates this: 'Whether you think you are a winner or a loser, remember you are right.'

"Take the example of a man who has always wanted to be self-employed. He may know he could handle it, but losing the security of a regular pay check gives him doubts. He feels he would be risking too much to venture out alone. In his mind, he justifies staying where he is. All of this reinforces the fear that he can't make it. You can see how his thinking holds him back.

"It is said you should 'follow your bliss.' This means following the inspiration of your spiritual Self in order to find happiness and fulfillment. It doesn't mean forgetting about your responsibilities. They are always there and you need to take care of them. It means to listen to your inner guide that gives you the vision about how your life can be.

"Sometimes this 'inner voice' is hard to hear, but it is there. Your inner voice may say you need to leave a relationship, or it may simply say you have a right to be happy and not feel guilty about the choices you make in your life. Change the beliefs that hold you back.

"Let's see if we can uncover some of them."

I asked the class to write down all the negative words, phrases, and sentences they thought or said about themselves. They were to include any comments that were discounts or slights.

"Some examples might be, 'I can't do this,' 'I am fat,' and 'I am not smart enough.' Be sure to include phrases commonly said within sentences, such as 'if I don't screw up' or 'if only I could do such and such.' "

I paused as the class wrote their responses. When everyone was done,

I asked them to share what they had written.

Don volunteered to speak first. "For as long as I can remember, I have thought of myself as being stupid. I don't know if I say very much about it out loud, but I think it. It probably stems from when I was young and had a hard time with reading. I remember my brothers did better in school than I, which made me the worst in the family. I know I need to change this thinking. I am not the smartest person in the world, but I am not stupid."

I encouraged Don to take on a better view of himself. Others agreed.

Jane said she always doubted herself, too. "I think my biggest problem is not feeling hopeful about things. I tend to worry that everything will turn out badly. It can be either at work or at home. It doesn't matter. Is there anything I can do about this?"

"Yes, there is," I said. "Let's all participate in this next exercise. First, take your list of negative self-statements and draw a large 'X' across the paper. This is symbolic of your resolve to stop using them. Say to yourself firmly, 'I won't be saying or thinking these anymore!'

"Now, turn your papers over and write the word 'Affirmations' at the top. We will compose three of them."

AFFIRMATIONS

"Simply put, affirmations are positive statements about yourself that affirm or give you support. They may talk about your positive qualities or encourage your efforts when you try to accomplish something. Examples are 'I can do this,' 'I will succeed,' and 'I am smart.'

"Affirmations can be said to yourself or they can be written down. If you write them out, display them in a room that you frequently walk into so they can be repeated often. For example, tape a list of your affirmations on a bathroom mirror. Whenever you are in your bathroom, say the affirmations out loud and let them sink in for a moment.

"Because anything in your environment becomes unnoticed after a few days, make a new list of affirmations and change its location. Then they will be fresh and continue to influence you.

"There are some guidelines I would like to give you for making useful affirmations. It is better to make them short and specific. Form the sentences using the first-person pronoun 'I' or the word 'my.' For example, an affirmation written this way might read, 'I will be calm and composed during my work presentation' or 'My work skills are good.' Use the present tense, such as 'I am a good person.'

"You can use the terms 'growing' or 'developing' for skills you are just beginning to learn. Then, after a few days, rewrite the affirmation as though the desired characteristic is already present. For example, you could say, 'I am growing more patient every day.' Then change it to 'I am patient.'

"When you compose your affirmations, avoid comparisons with other people or circumstances, such as 'I am better than John in my work,' or 'My house is better than Bob's.' Also, try not to use the words 'not' or 'never,' such as 'I don't look so bad.' Instead, say 'I am good-looking.' You can use 'no' for prohibitions such as 'no sugar' or 'no alcohol.'

"It is important to make your affirmations believable. For example, if someone is overweight, an affirmation that says 'I am thin' would not be helpful. Better affirmations would be 'I am attractive,' or 'I am reducing the fat content in the foods I eat,' or 'I will exercise three times a week.'

"Tailor your affirmations to refer to specific ways you feel about yourself. Look at your list of negative self-statements and use it as a guide to make positive ones.

"Let's consider an example. Don, may I use you? Your thoughts about being stupid can be counteracted through affirmations. "

Don agreed, and I asked him to listen to a few affirmations and decide which one he liked the best.

"You can say 'I am smart,' 'I am intelligent,' 'I am smart in many things,' 'I am resourceful,' or 'I can learn anything.'

Don answered, "I think the best one is 'I am resourceful and can learn many things.' It seems to be the most accurate."

"Good. Write it down on your paper," I told him.

"The part of the mind that affirmations affect is your body mind, or what is sometimes referred to as your unconscious or subconscious. It makes no judgments about what it lets in. It accepts everything. As I said before, it is like a sponge. Because of this, the more you repeat your affirmations, the greater the impact they will have on you. If you say them with strong feelings of conviction, their influence will increase even more."

Lisa shared, "I had a girlfriend whose brothers always said she was homely. She was really cute, and I could never understand why they said that. My friend was so influenced by it that she couldn't get the idea out of her head. She always thought she was ugly."

"That is an example of how the body mind can be swayed to accept anything it hears," I said. "It needs guidance. It is like a car you drive. If a car doesn't have a driver, it can cause a lot of destruction. The same is true with negative thoughts about yourself. They can cause a lot of damage to your self-esteem.

"The driver of the car is your consciousness aided by your intelligence. It allows you to see what you are doing. It helps you realize you can *decide* how you want to treat yourself. You can eliminate negative thinking patterns and put your body mind in the back seat. Then the influence of your spiritual Self can help you 'drive' your thoughts and interactions in the world.

"Remember, you are the *consciousness* behind your thinking. You, as a *being*, receive information from your world. You are more than just your feelings and thoughts. You, as a being, reside in your physical body and use your feelings to tell you things about your environment.

"Instead of the words 'I am hungry,' a more accurate statement is 'My body is hungry.' Instead of 'I am angry,' the more accurate statement is 'My emotions are angry.' Looking at your feelings this way gives you more self-determination in how you live your life.

"You don't have to be a slave to your emotions. You can decide how you want to feel. Just watch your feelings and make a choice.

"Take an example of a mother whose baby is teething. The child's irritability is understood by the mother who knows sore gums are painful. She may feel frustrated, but because she understands why the child is acting the way it is, she decides to feel patience and tolerance.

"It may not seem the mother is making a conscious choice about which emotions to have. Her response may seem automatic. In reality, it is both. The mother intuitively knows her baby cannot help being cranky when he doesn't feel good. She also wants to be a good mother, so she decides to accept the situation without getting upset.

"Let us look at a more difficult example in which you choose your feelings. Suppose you are driving in heavy traffic and a car cuts in front of you so suddenly you have to slam on your brakes to avoid an accident. You naturally feel irritated. Here is the decision point. You can let your annoyance go, or you can honk at the driver to let him or her know you are angry.

"Can anyone come up with other examples that illustrate the same point?"

"I think I have one," Al offered. "My wife brought a dessert to a potluck dinner at our church. She overheard someone complaining about how caloric it was. My wife normally tends to get a little sensitive about things like this, but because she knew the person who complained was very anxious about her weight, she decided not to take it personally."

"Yes, Al," I said, "that is an occasion where your wife decided to feel understanding of the person rather than feel criticized. Does anyone else have an example?"

"I do," Jane said. "My sister did not call me after some surgery I had. I felt hurt because it seemed she didn't care about me. I knew she was busy with her children, so I decided to call her to find out how she was doing. She was so sorry she hadn't called. She was stressed over some things that were happening at her job. She kept repeating her apology. I began to feel sorry for her because she felt so guilty. That made it easy for me to let go of my hurt."

"Thanks. These stories show how you make a choice about what kind of emotional reaction you will have in a difficult situation. It isn't easy to be accepting. It just takes practice.

"Be sure and use your affirmations this next week!"

NOTES
1. Awo Fa'lokun Fatunmbi, *Iba'se Orisa* (New York: Original Publications, 1994), p. 23.
2. Serge King, *Kahuna Healing* (Wheaton, Illinois: Theosophical Publishing House, 1983), pp. 126–27.
3. Quoted from a presentation by Native American lecturer Jamie Sams, at the Women of Wisdom Conference, Seattle, Washington, February 17, 1997.

The Spiritual Self

LEVELS OF CONSCIOUSNES

Personal Self	Physical Body and Body Mind
	Emotional Body
	Lower Mental Body — *This is the everyday mind.*
Spiritual Self	Higher Mental Body — *This is the part of the mind that receives intuition and utilizes reason and wisdom.*
	Intuitional Body
	Field of Unity

"Your spiritual Self is within you all the time. It is what gives you the feeling that you are alive. It unites your physical, emotional, and mental bodies to produce a whole. It is the sense of awareness that you have throughout your entire life, from childhood to adulthood, in sickness and health, in happiness and sadness.

"Your spiritual Self is timeless. It does not change with time. It is the part of you that looked out of your eyes at the world when you were a child and a teenager. It is the same as you see the world now that you're an adult.

"You may have a sense that, deep inside, you have been the same age all along. This is your spiritual Self. It is neither young nor old. It is ageless. It is through the spiritual Self that you have an awareness of the present, or the 'Now.'

"The spiritual Self does not die. It lives forever. It comes directly from the Source, which is of infinite duration. Courage in an individual is a quality of the immortal spiritual Self, which knows itself to be deathless and indestructible.

"A human being has been compared to a light bulb. The light bulb represents the physical body. Electricity runs through it to make it glow. The electricity is a metaphor for the spark of the Divine within you. The 'light' shining from the 'light bulb' comes from your spiritual Self. This is what makes your face light up when you meet a friend or when you smile at a baby. It is the 'light' from your 'heart.'

"When the sun shines on an object, shadows appear. These shadows are a metaphor for the problems that arise in your day-to-day life. When your consciousness gets buried in emotions, such as defensiveness or anger, the 'light' of your spiritual Self dims.

"The shadows represent the mistaken idea that your body and personality are all that you are. Spiritual teachers say to look away from the shadows. If you realize that you are the being behind your body and personality, then your personal problems will not have such a hold on you. You will be able to handle them with less difficulty.

"Another metaphor that describes this tells you to keep your face to the sunshine so the shadows fall behind you.

"An expression I heard from my grandmother says the same thing: 'If you keep your vision elevated, then your chin will automatically be kept up.' When your vision is elevated, you are looking at the world from the optimism that springs from your spiritual Self."

"Why we can't live in the spiritual Self all the time?" asked Lisa.

"This is due to your nature as a human being," I said. "In order to live in a physical body, spiritual consciousness must become consolidated and dense. The energy of the spiritual Self is vibrating too fast to exist on the physical plane. It needs the personal self and the physical body to 'gear it down,' so to speak.

"You have problems when your consciousness gets hung up at the emotional and mental levels and is unaware of the spiritual part of yourself. This is why it is referred to as hidden. It is always there, but when you are wrapped up in the concerns of your personal self, it is not in your awareness. Emotions of stress or worry cause you to have even less awareness of your spiritual nature, as if a light were covered by thick blankets.

"Just as a pearl grows within an oyster, the spiritual Self expands within the personal self. A grain of sand inside its shell irritates the oyster. This prompts the oyster to turn the sand into a pearl.

"The same is true with your personal self. As you encounter life's irritations, you develop understanding about how to handle them. You learn patience, strength, and wisdom. These are your 'pearls.' It is only through living life with its joys as well as its sorrows that you can learn to express the qualities of your spiritual Self."

"How can a person be more in tune with the spiritual Self?" Al asked.

"This is done by quieting your personal self," I answered. "You turn away from the thoughts and emotions that occupy you on a mundane level. You let them go. This is what is meant by the expression, 'In order to find your Self, you need to lose your self.'

"Detaching from your personal self is also spoken of in the beautiful Prayer of St. Francis of Assisi. In the last line, he refers to the self 'dying.' The prayer reads:

"Lord, make me an instrument of thy peace.
"Where there is hatred, let me sow love;
"Where there is injury, pardon;
"Where there is doubt, faith;
"Where there is despair, hope;
"Where there is darkness, light;
"Where there is sadness, joy.

"O divine Master, grant that I may not so much seek
"To be consoled as to console,

"To be understood as to understand,

"To be loved as to love;

"For it is in giving that we receive;

"It is in pardoning that we are pardoned;

"It is in dying [of the self] that we are born to eternal life.

"An example of a time when you let go of the interests of your personal self is when you experience laughter. When you laugh, you are unaware of your problems and concerns. You naturally open to your spiritual Self.

"Native Americans refer to this when they say laughter is the natural call of the human being. I'm sure you have heard it said that every animal has its own call. For example, the call of the wolf is its howl. This is how it connects with other wolves. The essence of the wolf is communicated this way.

"For the human 'animal,' you might think its call would be speech, but it isn't. It is laughter which makes a true connection to another human being through the light of the Self."

Lisa chuckled and said, "This makes me think of the feeling of oneness I have when I get together with my sisters and we all start laughing about something. Any disagreements we have had in the past are all forgotten at that moment. Everything is forgiven."

"That is so true. I have even felt this with my ex-husband," offered Jane.

"I'm sure you all know the laughter we are speaking of is not laughing *at* anyone, but *with* someone, where a sense of unity is felt," I said. "If you laugh at someone, it is an attempt to feel good by putting someone else down. This is because the personal self wants to feel better than another. Again, you automatically let go of your personal self when you laugh because it has the component of love.

"Patanjali was a spiritual teacher in India around the fourth century B.C.E. He compared the spiritual Self to beautiful music being played on a piano by a talented musician. The keys on the piano symbolize the physical body and the emotions. The musician is the mind, using the piano to express the harmony and melody of the spiritual Self.

"As you know, a piano can be pounded on or played poorly, just like the personal self can display anger or selfishness. But the talented musician playing wonderful music is the same as you expressing qualities of love and kindness. These are expressions of the unity of all.

"The spiritual Self is referred to in many ways. St. Theresa called it the 'Interior Castle.' The Biblical saying 'the Kingdom of Heaven is within you' is another reference. It has been described as the Holy Grail, which symbolizes a cup holding the spiritual Self. Plato referred it as the 'nous.'

"Because the spiritual Self needs vehicles through which to express itself, it must use your personal self — your thoughts, feelings, and actions. For example, it flows through your mind as reason, wisdom, and intuition. It expresses itself through emotions of love, kindness, and the feeling of oneness with nature. Finally, it is displayed in the complex and intricate functioning of your physical body and the instincts of your body mind."

I took out my easel and said, "Let's brainstorm other qualities of your spiritual Self which you manifest through your personal self."

This is the list we made.

EXPRESSIONS OF YOUR SPIRITUAL SELF
THROUGH YOUR PERSONAL SELF

The Personal Self	**Expressions of the Spiritual Self**
Physical body	the immune system
	reflexes
	muscle strength
	natural painkillers from the brain
	cell growth and repair
	the five senses, sense of direction
	expressions in art
	the will to live, the survival instinct
	caution, alertness
Emotional body	forgiveness, compassion
	tenderness, mercy, kindness
	affection, love, devotion, commitment
	sympathy, warmth

	courtesy, gentleness
	humor
	generosity
	patience, tolerance
Mental body	reason, intelligence, understanding
	conviction, purpose
	common sense, memory
	thoughtfulness, empathy
	wisdom, insight, intuition
	discretion, judgment, caution
	tact, diplomacy
	cleverness
	abstract thinking

"A wonderful quote from Meister Eckhart refers to the spiritual Self manifesting through the personal self in compassion. He wrote, 'Compassion clothes the soul with the robe of God and divinely adorns it.'[1]"

"Sue, can you talk a bit about intuition and how it works?" asked Al.

INTUITION

"I'd be happy to," I said. "I am sure all of you have experienced intuition at one point or another. As you know, intuition refers to the knowledge and understanding of things beyond that which you have been taught. It is the direct perception of truth. This is knowledge you come by instinctively.

"Intuition helps you in many ways. It guides your thinking when you need to solve a problem. It keeps you on the right track. It helps you draw useful conclusions. It gives you a sense of perspective and the ability to see into things, or *in-sight*.

"Each of you has probably experienced the effect of intuition in your life. Would anyone like to share such an incident with the class?"

After a pause, Jane spoke up. "I was very close to my grandmother. She loved a certain lilac perfume which she always seemed to wear. If I went over to her house, she would put some on me, too. Her closet smelled of lilacs and she even had a lilac bush in her yard.

"After she died, there were several times I would be thinking of her when, out of nowhere, I smelled the fragrance of lilacs. It was just like her perfume! One time was at her funeral. I smelled it so strongly I thought someone had actually worn the same perfume.

"Another time was a few months later at her grave. No one else was there but me, so I knew the smell had not come from another person. Looking back on those times, I realized that I was not actually smelling her perfume, but somehow connecting to her in such a way that made the smell seem real. Was this at the level of intuition?"

"Yes, I think it was," I told her. "That is a wonderful story, Jane. Thank you for sharing it. Does anyone else have an example of intuition?"

"At times," Jim offered, "my job involves a fair amount of writing. I may have to write personnel policies or other information that goes out to the staff. Sometimes, I am at a loss for words. That is when I find myself just sitting at my computer and thinking.

"I start writing a sentence and let my mind open to the subject. Pretty soon, a solution comes. It is interesting how this works. I think it is an example of using my intuition to solve a problem that is stumping me."

"You're right, Jim, it is," I said. "That is a good suggestion if any of us are stuck in the same way. Can anyone think of another example?"

"I have one," Anne volunteered. "We have a dog at home, which I absolutely adore. Her name is Lucky. I know what she is feeling just by looking at her. I can see her moods in her expressions — when she is happy to see me or sad she has to stay home. I can tell if she isn't feeling well or if she is tired. Probably the most important feeling I pick up is her devotion and loyalty to me and my family. She is a very loving dog."

"That is a wonderful example, Anne," I said. "Understanding animals and other things in nature comes through our intuition. Physical cues can give you an idea of what an animal is experiencing, but you know you are right from your intuition. Would anyone else like to share?"

"When I met my wife," Al began, "I fell deeply in love. I was in college and when I couldn't be with her, I took to writing poetry. It wasn't very good, but I felt inspired to try and put my feelings into words."

"Good for you, Al," I said. "I'm sure your wife enjoyed it. I would like to share an experience that happened to me a long time ago. I was driving home from work one summer evening and was about three blocks from my home. I was relaxed and driving my car somewhat automatically, not thinking of anything in particular.

"Suddenly, I had this image of a child, riding a scooter across the road in front of my car. It was so real, I put on my brakes and slowed down. It was lucky I did, because right before my eyes, a child darted into the street. It was the same child on a scooter that I had just pictured in my mind! He came out from between some trees at the side of the road. It happened so fast I surely would have hit him had I not already been applying my brakes. I was so grateful for that moment of inspiration. I would have hated to have had an accident.

"Another story describes how information is communicated through the intuitional plane. It is referred to as 'The 100th Monkey'[2] and is from a book of the same name by Ken Keyes, Jr. In his book, Keyes describes the observations of scientists studying Japanese monkeys on an island called Koshima in 1952. Scientists provided sweet potatoes to the monkeys by dropping them in the sand. The monkeys liked the sweet potatoes, but didn't like the sand and dirt that got mixed in with them.

"A solution was found by an eighteen-month-old female monkey named Imo. She started washing her sweet potatoes in a nearby stream. Imo taught her mother to wash the sand off, too. Gradually, through observation and imitation, other monkeys learned to wash the dirt off their food. Over several years, this practice spread widely over the island.

"Not all the monkeys washed their sweet potatoes, however. The only monkeys who learned to do this were those in close association with the monkeys who did.

"All of a sudden, something startling occurred. In 1958, scientists discovered all the monkeys on Koshima were washing their sweet potatoes, even if they had not been around other monkeys who had this skill. In looking into this, they discovered monkeys on other islands were also washing the sand off their food. It seemed apparent to the scientists that knowledge about this new behavior was being communicated in some other fashion than through one monkey copying the behavior of another.

"How did this happen? Ken Keyes theorized that when enough monkeys had learned to wash their sandy sweet potatoes — say ninety-nine of them — there was enough mental energy created about the behavior that the hundredth monkey picked up the idea through a communication directly into his mind. His theory said that the intensity of the thought-form itself was powerful enough to communicate the idea to the rest of the monkeys through the mental plane alone.

"This experience makes the point that when a new awareness is shared by enough people, the mental field is strengthened to such a degree that almost everyone picks up the same idea. The monkeys learning to wash their sweet potatoes is an example of how evolution takes place. When new and better ways to live your life are implemented, it exerts an influence on everyone to participate."

YOUR INNER VOICE

"Intuition is an aspect of your spiritual Self. It has also been referred to as 'the little voice inside' which knows the right thing to do. When you think something is about to happen and you have the sense of what it will be, the spiritual Self is shedding light to illuminate it. This is what is meant when you say, 'In my heart I knew.' It is also what gives you prophetic dreams.

"I'm going to lead you through an exercise designed to help you ask for guidance from your spiritual Self. I refer to it as your 'inner voice.' It can give you insight about the underlying causes of your feelings and why they trouble you. Take out a piece of paper and a pencil so you can write down any discoveries you make."

I first led the class through a brief meditation so they could clear their minds of the day's events. After that, I asked everyone to settle into a state of "no mind," which is a mind that is thinking of nothing.

"Reflect on a problem area that you would like some insight about. Allow it to come into your mind.

"Be aware of your feelings about the problem, but don't start thinking about it in your usual way. Allow yourself to simply experience your reactions, fully and completely.

"If you have a physical sensation accompanying this, such as a tight stomach or the urge to cry, allow it to happen. Simply observe what you are experiencing for a few minutes.

"Now, let one feeling in particular that you would like to understand come up into your awareness."

"Ask your inner voice to give you some clues about why you feel this specific way. Are you afraid of something? Is there a lesson for you to learn from it?

"It may be easier to start a sentence and wait for your intuition to finish it, such as 'I feel worried about this because I fear. . . .' Wait patiently for your answer.

"If you feel comfortable with this process, go ahead and ask yourself a series of questions. You might want to delve into some of the underlying causes of the problem.

"When you have had enough time with your inner dialogue, come back to the room and open your eyes.

"How was this experience for you?"

Jim spoke up first. "This is similar to what I do when I am stuck in my writing process at work. Just now, I wanted some help on a problem I am having there. I have a member of my staff who does excellent work, but has some personality problems that interfere with his getting along with others. I asked for help in figuring out a plan for him to work on his relationships with others."

"I'd be interested to hear what you came up with for this employee, if you feel okay talking about it," Lisa said.

Jim nodded and answered, "Sure. I think I will refer him to a counselor, such as Sue, for his own insights into why he gets so stressed-out. I decided it is a good time for an outside trainer to come in for an all-staff in-service on stress management. I also think, in his yearly review, I will list some specific behaviors for him to improve in his relations with the other staff. During this exercise, I was able to pinpoint some of those areas."

"That's very good," I said. "Do others of you want to share what you learned?"

Anne hesitantly voiced her comments. "In this meditation, I wanted some insights about what to do with my daughters. They are both teenagers and seem to be getting more and more hostile toward me. I worry I am too strict, but I don't want to give them too much freedom all at once.

"What I discovered with this exercise is that I am doing fine with what I am expecting of them, but I need to give them more leeway as to when they do it. To give you an example, I don't need to be so particular about how soon they finish their chores. They are both good girls. They study hard and get along with each other. I don't want to mess this up. It seems I don't need to worry so much about it."

Don said, "Isn't that the advice all parents need for teenagers? My kids say I should have done more of that when they were growing up."

"How did the exercise work for you, Don?" I asked.

"I wanted some insight about how to handle my mother," Don answered. "I won't go into all the problems I am having with her now — it would take hours. She is still living on her own, but has some health problems I have had to deal with. She may need to go into a nursing home. I realized that just now. I also decided not to feel guilty about it."

"Good for you, Don," said Jim.

"Is the spiritual Self the same as your conscience?" Al asked.

YOUR CONSCIENCE

"Yes, but it depends upon what you mean by 'conscience,' " I said. "The word can refer to different things. It can be thought of as the aspect of your spiritual Self that helps you distinguish right from wrong. For example, it holds you back from hurting someone. Your conscience helps you live in harmony with others.

"There is another way that conscience is viewed, however. It can refer to the training you receive from your parents and the society in which you live. This is conditioning about what is considered proper behavior in your culture. It may or may not harmonize with your spiritual Self. Let me explain.

"There are various rules of social conduct that oblige you to act in certain ways, such as being courteous and considerate of others. This is in accordance with the spiritual Self, which knows the Oneness of all.

"Other rules of society teach people to act in accordance with tradition. These include, among other things, dating behavior, how to discipline children, and marriage customs. These differ from generation to generation and from culture to culture. They use guilt and other means to control people's behavior.

"The guidelines for proper behavior may be completely unrelated to what is in harmony with the spiritual Self. For example, a girl may feel guilty for eating a dessert and say she has a 'guilty conscience.' Another example is someone feeling guilty for taking a vacation when there is work to be done. These are cases where people have been conditioned to feel a certain way, rather than being truly influenced by the spiritual Self.

"The search for guidance from the spiritual Self has always been important for societies and cultures around the world. It is the topic of fables and stories that have been passed down throughout the ages. Because the spiritual Self cannot easily be described with words, metaphor and other symbolism have been used to help describe the process.

"*The Arabian Nights* is one such set of stories. It is a collection of Eastern folk tales from Indian and Persian sources, gathered between the tenth and twelfth centuries C.E. It includes 'Ali Baba and the Forty Thieves,' 'Sinbad the Sailor,' and 'Aladdin.'

"One story tells about a farmer who is plowing his field. His plow gets caught in a tangle of roots. When he digs into the earth to free his plow, he finds a gold ring. He digs even deeper and finds a cave. Going deep within the cave, he uncovers a treasure chest of precious jewels.

"The meaning of this story is multi-faceted. The plow getting stuck in the tangle of roots in the ground represents all the unresolved feelings and issues in the 'shadow side' of your personality. This refers to traits your may not be conscious of and probably don't want to examine. These feelings and issues cause personality problems and other conflicts in your life.

"This is where your work is. You must dig deeply within yourself for insight into how and why you act the way you do.

"The gold ring encourages you in this process. It is a reward for directly confronting your psychological issues without letting your defenses sway you into blaming someone or something else for your problems and shortcomings.

"If you examine yourself thoroughly and honestly, you will find a reward. You reach the cave, which is the quiet mind, or the opening to your spiritual Self. Then you are rewarded with a treasure of jewels, which is Self-realization.

"Greek mythology has many stories that symbolize the struggle we face in overcoming the selfish tendencies of our personal selves. One symbol is the Minotaur, which is a monster with the head of a bull and the body of a man. This represents the self-centered qualities of the personal self. It can cause a person to act bull-headed — like an animal.

"The Minotaur kills and devours other humans who are in a labyrinth. The labyrinth represents day-to-day life on the physical plane. It is like a maze in that your purpose for being here is puzzling and unclear. You will have many struggles before you realize how to live as an expression of your spiritual Self.

"The word 'personality' comes from the Latin 'persona.' This refers to the theatrical masks worn long ago by Greek actors in plays. The word 'sona' means 'sound.' 'Per' refers to 'through.' The actors spoke sound, through their masks.

"The mask symbolizes the personality, which is what the spiritual Self must use or 'speak through' when it functions on the physical plane. Just as the actors used the masks to perform, you use your body and personality to live in the world.

"The point of this metaphor is the realization that you are not the mask. You are much more than your body and personality. You are a spirit using your body and personality to function and evolve.

"Granted, this is easy to forget. It is natural to think of yourself as a set of characteristics identifying your personal self, such as your sex or age. But, if you do, you are identifying with things that are time-limited. Your body grows old and dies. So does your personality. It is gone when your body dies. But your spirit is unlimited. It doesn't die or fade away. It is everlasting.

"Identifying yourself with your body will cause you to be unhappy, because the body is never how you want it to be. It doesn't have a perfect shape. If it does, with time it changes. Neither does the body perform as you want. You always want it to do better. Finally, the body deteriorates, grows old, and wears out. It doesn't last forever.

"Realizing this allows you to see that you cannot find happiness through anything physical. Happiness comes from non-physical things, such as enjoying someone's company or having loving family relationships. The elements you enjoy are love and the feeling of unity, which come through your spiritual Self.

"Identifying with your body can lead you to want cosmetic surgery. But let me ask you a question. Do you like a woman better if she has had a face lift? No. She is still the same person inside.

"If someone is in an auto accident and suffers facial scarring from injuries, you don't feel differently about him. You still like him because of the essence of who he is. You enjoy the spirit of the person. How he looks is secondary.

"A Native American expression refers to this. It speaks to the futility of measuring your value based on your looks. It says, 'The antelope doesn't fear coming up short next to a daffodil.' The outer covering of a person is unimportant."

"But in our society, looks are important," Jane said.

Al countered, "That's because we have been trained to look at people from the outside. There is so much advertising about wearing stylish clothes, being in shape, and appearing young. But, as the saying goes, 'Beauty is only skin deep.' "

"Well said," I agreed. "The personal self is yours for only a short time. At the end of your life, you shed it. It is like a shirt you put on. Just as you change your shirt at the end of the day, you change your physical body at the end of your lifetime. At the start of your next life, you take on a new one. This is why it is meaningless to identify with your personal self.

"Nothing on earth can be considered yours. Your property was someone else's before you owned it. In the future, it will belong to yet another person. When you take a seat in a restaurant, you think of it as your seat. But when you leave, you don't take the seat with you. In life, things come and go. You only have them for a short time.

"The same is true with children. Your child is 'yours' while he is your responsibility, but he grows up to become his own person. The only thing you have is your spiritual Self.

"A Buddhist phrase describes the reason you have problems in life when you identify with your personal self. This is due to 'dust covering your eyes.' When you realize the true nature of your spiritual Self, you remove the 'dust' and see the truth about who you are."

"So, if we are not supposed to identify with the characteristics of our personal self, such as our minds and our bodies, what are we supposed to do with them when we are living on the physical plane? Is it wrong to want to learn things?" Lisa questioned.

"No, it is entirely natural to want to learn and understand things in life," I answered. "The point is to not identify yourself with them. It isn't useful to think of yourself as someone who is smart or knowledgeable on this or that. You are a spiritual being. You are more than what you do with your mind.

"The same idea applies to other aspects of your personal self. Don't identify yourself with your body or your emotions, either. These are simply vehicles which you, the spiritual being, use. You need to take care of them, but not let them define you. They are limited. You are more than a set of attributes, such as gender, race, age, size, IQ, or temperament. These are totally inadequate to describe the real you."

Anne thought to herself that she knew this lesson well. She had learned it the hard way. It all started when she decided to have cosmetic surgery for breast implants. Because of problems that resulted, Anne sank into a depression that was the stimulus for her to seek counseling.

Anne's body rejected the breast implants, forcing their removal. She also suffered other complications which caused some scarring and disfigurement. Anne ultimately felt she was in worse shape than before she had the surgery.

Through counseling, Anne realized her self-esteem was centered around how she looked. Inside, she felt deficient. When she dealt with this, she faced feelings of inadequacy that had begun in her childhood.

Gradually, Anne developed a healthier self-image that relied on her inner qualities, rather than her physical attributes. With self-acceptance came a sense of perspective about what was important to her. She learned what mattered was on the inside of a person.

This was hard to develop. Anne had to face a sense of loss over what she felt was her femininity. She had to overcome the feeling that she was less than whole because of the changes in her body after the surgery. She realized if she identified herself with her body, she would feel lacking. If she identified herself as the being using her body to live, it would help her resolve feelings of inadequacy and disappointment.

It took awhile for Anne to integrate these ideas into her thinking. She had to change her entire way of perceiving herself. This could only be accomplished over time. Eventually, she learned to accept her body once again and view it in its proper perspective.

Jim had been a constant support for Anne. He hadn't thought she needed the surgery in the first place. He loved her no matter how her body looked. He pointed out that, because no one knew about her scars, any feelings of being defective came from within herself.

Anne decided the changes in her body as a result of her surgery would serve to remind her that her identity did not come from how she looked, but from who she was. She learned to identify with this rather than her body.

The class discussion had turned into one that focused on relationships. Jane asked, "What happens when you fall in love? Are you expressing your spiritual Self then?"

"What do you think, Jane?" I asked.

LOVE

"I think when you fall in love, you must be functioning with your spiritual Self," Jane responded. "Everything seems to be perfect. You trust the other person and bend over backwards to please him. You show your love by buying presents or being helpful. It is so sad this idyllic existence has to end. Why is that?"

"Good question!" I said. "Understanding this is one of the secrets of life. I agree with you, Jane. It's too bad we don't always act in loving ways.

Relationships don't work for different reasons, but looking at a few common factors will help us understand why problems arise.

"When you fall in love, you are very open to your spiritual Self. You feel a oneness with the other person. You experience a sense of unity. The reason this ends is the influence of your personal self.

"Your personal self wants things to be a certain way. It wants the love relationship to make you feel special and complete all the time. If this doesn't happen, it looks for someone to blame. This can create conflicts or cause the person to withdraw.

"The personal self doesn't want to accept things simply as they are. It may influence you to try and change your partner. It is geared to going after what it feels will make you happy. It watches out for your interests only. Unless you are aware of this, it can overshadow the love and acceptance inspired by your spiritual Self.

"The personal self can also undermine a relationship because of the influence of fear. Let me give you some examples. After you fall in love and feel a strong sense of connection with your loved one, the personal self can kick in and fear it will end. It can make you want to hold on to the other person and become possessive. You may feel jealous if your loved one wants to do something without you, or you worry that he or she doesn't love you anymore.

"To protect yourself, you may hold back from being open and natural. Tension can come between the two of you. This only reinforces your fears, and adds to the strain and defensiveness. Unless you realize what is happening and work against the barriers that have been built, the relationship can end.

"Only by using your intelligence can you recognize this. You have to develop your awareness so you can see when your personal self is controlling you. The personal self needs you to guide it.

"You are in the driver's seat. You use the reactions from your personal self only to give you information. Then you evaluate the situation by using your intelligence and the influence of your higher mind to see if you want be concerned about it.

"This way, you do more than just react to what is going on. Reactions come from the personal self with its strong self-interest. As you know, this is driven by the self-centeredness of the survival instinct. When you use your intelligence, you decide how you want to *act*, rather than *react* to circumstances.

"In any relationship, there are bound to be problems to resolve. No two people live in exactly the same fashion. Each person has different needs and wants. The key is to find ways to work out your differences with the love from your spiritual Self.

"Love is an extension of the plane of Unity. It is an awareness of the oneness of all. It manifests in many ways. Let me give you some examples.

"First of all, love brings about attraction between a man and a woman. It is the basis of the desire for union. Love also is displayed in sympathy, which is the feeling of concern for another that you would have for yourself. It is evident in sacrifice, which is giving to another without thinking of yourself.

"Love brings about understanding of other people. When you know someone well enough to understand him, you have unified with him and can see the world through his eyes.

"Love springs spontaneously from within. It is a manifestation of your spiritual Self. It awakens love in another. It is irresistible. Nothing can conquer it. It will not be extinguished.

"The power of love is transformative. It can be used to transform yourself or show confidence in another person's ability to change.

"All emotions are variations of love, even the 'negative' emotions of hate or jealousy. Let me explain how this is so. The 'positive' expressions of love have a quality that is outgoing to another. There is a desire to give. The giving can be expressed physically through touch, words, or facial expressions. It can also be unspoken, as in sympathy and understanding.

"The 'negative' expressions of love direct the giving to oneself and attempt to deny others of it. Examples are possessiveness and envy. In possessiveness, you want to be the only one to possess something. You don't want to share it with others. You love what you have and feel you will lose it if it is shared.

"Envy is the love of what someone else has, such as success, friends, or possessions. You feel discontented with your situation. You envy someone who has more of something you would love to have.

"In the fourteenth century, Dante, the inspired Italian poet, wrote *The Divine Comedy*. In this work, he maintained that too much love is the source of all evil. He said that love becomes evil when it is expressed in a way that is perverted, weakened, or defective.

"For example, Dante described how the love of justice, when perverted, leads to revenge. Love of yourself, if weakened, can lead to love of someone's else good fortune, or covetousness. A weakened love of yourself can cause pride and the feeling that you are better than others.

"Dante said that sloth is love that is defective, in that you don't love something in its proper proportion. This is where you love relaxing so much that you become lazy, or you have too much love of food, resulting in overeating.

"These 'negative' expressions of love are the reasons Dante said 'love has teeth.' Love can separate and divide one from another as well as bring about harmony and union."

"What is it when a person puts someone else down to make himself feel better? Is that perverted love?" asked Jane.

Al offered, "I used to work with someone who did that all the time. His comments always seemed to undercut someone who was doing better than him."

"That can happen," I agreed. "It is an example of how the personal self can override good sense. Reason tells you that putting someone down doesn't make you any better. But the personal self may try to do it anyway. You need to watch yourself and curb these tendencies."

"Can you talk about the different ways to show love?" Don asked.

"There are many different expressions of love," I said. "They vary in proportion with the amount of giving you extend to another. There is only a mild degree of giving to someone else when you show respect and courtesy. This is the extent to which love is expressed between strangers, for example.

"Kindness has a deeper degree of giving. Tenderness has even more. Friendship can involve a wide range of expression depending upon the nature of the relationship. There may be only a mild degree of giving between some friends, while another set of friends may share deep love and affection."

"What about worship, or the love of God?" Al asked.

"In worship, you long for union with the object of your worship. You want to merge with it," I said. "You give up yourself and your personal wants and needs. You take on the will of whomever or whatever you are worshipping, rather than rely on your own will.

"In worshipping a deity or God, you try to embody the characteristics the deity represents. These usually are the 'positive' expressions of love. However, if you worship a political leader who doesn't advocate harmony and love, you may be compelled to serve in an army that oppresses its subjects. You give up your ability to choose."

Al commented, "This reminds me of the mass suicides by a few religious groups we have heard about on the news in the last several years. These seem to be examples where the will of the individuals in the group was turned over to the leader."

"Yes, the followers may have thought they were worshipping God by killing themselves," I said. "But in reality, they were worshipping their leader. They merged with him and took on his beliefs."

"How can this happen with love?" asked Lisa.

"It can happen because relationships that have the component of worship also have an imbalance of power between the two parties," I explained. "This is where problems can arise. Worship strives to neutralize the imbalance of power to bring about a sense of union through the way love is expressed.

"Annie Besant, in her book *A Study in Consciousness*, described this when she wrote, 'Love looking downward is benevolence. Love looking upward is reverence. Love among equals is desire for mutual help. Hate looking downward is scorn. Hate looking upward is fear. Hate among equals is mutual injury.'[3]

"Friendship is a form of love expressed by people who are relatively equal to one another. It differs from the love expressed when there is an unequal relationship, such as between a parent and a child. The parent shows the child love through kindness and caring because the child is dependent upon the parent. The child gives back through loyalty, respect, and devotion. It does what the parent wants.

"As the child matures and grow into an adult, it develops independence and makes its own decisions. The relationship changes and becomes more equal, with each person giving in a similar fashion. They can become friends, as well as remain parent and child."

"Isn't patriotism a form of love?" Don inquired. "Isn't it love of one's country?"

"Yes, patriotism is a form of brotherly love," I answered. " In patriotism, individuals join together for the common purpose of preserving their way of life. It shows brotherly love in that it embodies giving to all alike without favoring one person or another."

Jim said, "I am reminded of the expression, 'Love your neighbor as yourself.' This seems to me to describe brotherly love."

"And what about justice?" Lisa asked. "Doesn't that go with brotherly love?"

"Yes, you have all given good examples," I said. "The way justice displays love is through fairness and equality for everyone. These are ways you would want to treat your brother or someone close to you.

"Any form of love is an expression of your spiritual Self. It can be shown in various ways, such as through forgiveness, courtesy, or warmth. Expressing love is like 'sunshine to flowers.' It makes everything thrive.

"When you embody love in your interactions with others, relationships flourish. There is a sense of compatibility and accord. This is what is meant by the saying, 'Melody is our praise of God. Harmony is God's answer back to us.' "

EXPRESSIONS OF YOUR HEART

"Love is said to come from your heart. It comes from the core of your being. The heart is considered to be the organ for expressing the emotions of your spiritual Self. This is only natural in that your heart is also at the core of your physical existence. It is necessary for you to live. It pumps blood to nourish your entire system and is the central organ for life.

"Many expressions are said that associate your heart with feelings of love. Emotions expressing unity and love generally are referred to as 'heartfelt' emotions, such as loving kindness and sympathy. You may say you love a person from the 'bottom of your heart.' When you listen closely to someone in an effort to truly understand what he is saying, you are listening not only with your ears, but also 'with your heart.'

"If a loved one ends a relationship with you, you say your 'heart is broken.' If you change a negative opinion about something to one that is more positive, you have a 'change of heart.' Various other emotions are linked with the heart, such as 'warm-hearted,' 'cold-hearted,' and 'sick at heart.' Hate is said to 'cut the heart in two' or 'make it bleed.'

"The heart is also thought of as the place where you access your intuition. You know things intuitively from your 'heart.' Blaise Pascal, the French scientist and philosopher, said, 'The heart has its reasons which reason knows nothing of.'

"In addition to being thought of as the center of love and intuition, the heart is considered to be the source of your connection to the field of Unity. In meditation instruction, you are asked to center yourself within your heart. In the Bible, in Psalms 19:14, the same idea is expressed: 'Let the words of my mouth, and the meditation of my heart, be acceptable, O Lord.'

"This is also stated in another Bible verse from Matthew 5:8: 'Blessed are the pure in heart: for they shall see God.'

"Because of the many ways your heart is associated with your spiritual Self, I'd like to lead you through a brief meditation that centers within your heart.

"Let us feel harmony with the group.

"Let us feel harmony with nature.

"Think of someone you love. Open your heart and send love to him or her.

"Feel a deep sense of unity with all. Open your heart even wider and let it expand to include everything in the universe.

"Allow this openness to settle within you. Become one with it inside your heart.

"Open to your basic essence. Become one with it inside the cave of your heart. Experience the silence that is there.

"Thank you."

After a pause, I explained, "I wanted to lead you through a meditation focusing with your heart because it can make your meditation more complete. Meditation is so often focused within your head and mind. Opening your heart makes it a fuller experience.'

Lisa commented, "I enjoyed this way to meditate very much. I found it very deep and easier to hold on to rather than trying to clear my mind."

"I am glad you found it useful," I said.

"I liked thinking about the feeling of love," Al offered. "It was natural to experience it when you had us go into the cave of our hearts."

"Wonderful!" I said. "The love within you is limitless. It comes from a source that is beyond your personal self. I'm sure you have heard the expression, 'Your cup overfloweth.' Your heart is so full it overflows with love. The desire to have your love returned vanishes."

"What is the nature of hate?" Lisa asked. "I know it is the opposite of love, but can you shed some light on it? I am interested in knowing what to do if you feel hate."

"This is a useful topic to discuss," I said. "Hate is a feeling probably everyone has experienced. It is an emotion created in the body mind, and in your emotional and mental bodies. It is a defensive reaction resulting from feeling a loss of something you love, such as your self-esteem or physical well-being.

"If you are humiliated or degraded, you lose the sense that you deserve respect. It is easy to hate the person who made you feel this way. Likewise, if you are physically hurt, you lose your state of good health. You hate that which threatens your sense of safety.

"Hate serves the purpose of neutralizing your emotional state. It helps you vent painful emotions and return to a state of calm.

"For example, you may feel bad about yourself as a result of being physically abused. If you hate the person who treated you this way, you reject self-hate. You direct the hate outward, away from yourself. This allows you to have a sense of self-esteem without overtones of negativity. You can take care of yourself and reject the implication that somehow you deserved the unfair treatment. It is natural for you to want to feel worthy of love and consideration.

"The basis of hatred is not feeling whole. You don't feel good and you hate whatever made you feel that way. The way to relieve this is to do some of your personal 'work.' This means you try to understand what underlies your animosity. Instead of directing your feelings away from yourself when you hate, look within. Hate is like a veneer. It only covers more vulnerable feelings of pain.

"For example, you may hate your father for being critical and not showing you enough love and acceptance when you were growing up. You feel you would have developed a better sense of self-esteem and self-confidence if he hadn't been so strict and overpowering. Underneath your hate are feelings of being unacceptable and unlovable. These need to be transformed in order for you to feel better."

"Is it useful to confront the person you hate?" Lisa asked.

"Yes, sometimes it is helpful," I answered. "It depends upon the circumstances. Usually, you hate a person for doing something harmful to you that you were unable to overcome. This can happen when someone has authority over you. Examples are parents, teachers, or someone who threatens you with physical harm.

"After you have recovered from the experiences that caused your hate in the first place, it may be helpful to talk to the person about the effect his or her behavior had on you. For example, as an adult, you may want to express your feelings about past sexual abuse to the one who abused you.

"However, it is important to do this without speaking in a hateful way. Talk about the effects of the treatment you received and its impact on your life. Explaining how you were traumatized not only releases pent-up thoughts and feelings, but also equalizes your sense of power in relation to the other person.

"If you hate one of your parents, you were probably young when you started feeling that way. As a child, you internalized a view of yourself as powerless and helpless. When you bring up the matter to your parents when you are older, you speak from a position of strength and equality. This counteracts feelings of impotence and inadequacy. You feel more in control of your life."

"Is this all that has to be done?" Jane asked.

"No, it isn't," I said. "You still have more internal 'work' to do. You need to put your own efforts into not feeling bad about yourself for whatever happened. Holding on to painful feelings can become a habit. You must learn to value yourself and get your needs met.

"The greatest part of your work is within yourself. It may seem overwhelming, but it can be done. It might feel easier to hold on to your hate, but that keeps alive the underlying beliefs about your lack of worth. Eventually, you need to resolve all this and grow beyond what happened in the past."

Jane reflected, "Resolving something on your own has to be done anyway if the person you hate is no longer alive. For me, I wouldn't want to confront my father. I'd rather take care of my feelings alone."

"It is each individual's choice," I said. "Whatever works best for you is what you need to do."

"What about other reasons why a person hates?" queried Don. "It seems hate can come from jealousy."

"Yes, that is true," I said. "Jealousy results from feeling that you are inferior to the person you are jealous of. You believe you don't measure up. If you hate the person who makes you feel less worthy, you don't have to look at your own sense of inadequacy.

"Many times, people do not even know they are reacting from hate. They automatically reject the one who seems to be better than they are.

"Instead of directing your hate outward, analyze yourself to see what you feel inside. Think about whether you feel unworthy. This takes some uncovering, because your feelings are often protected by defensiveness. You have to peel them off gradually, like peeling the layers of an onion. At the center is probably a sense of inadequacy that you have had for a long time. This can all be resolved, but it takes persistence."

"It seems like there is so much work in life, like working on relationships or working on yourself, when all a person wants is to be happy," Jane complained.

"Well, I want more than just happiness," Don said jokingly. "I want some money to enjoy some of the good things in life, too."

DESIRE

"You're not alone. Let me talk a little about desire. It is a natural part of life. Desire is longing for things you think will make you happy. They may be material possessions or intangibles, such as power or security. With desire, you hope to gain other feelings you normally associate with happiness, such as peace, love, satisfaction, and contentment.

"For example, you desire calmness and contentment, so you seek a comfortable home and relaxing vacations. You desire love, so you look for a warm and caring relationship. You desire the feeling of wellness in your body, so you exercise and eat right to be healthy. You want to feel good.

"You don't realize it consciously, but you are looking for the qualities that epitomize your spiritual Self. The spiritual Self is the ultimate of peacefulness, love, and wholeness. The problem with this is you are looking for happiness by trying to satisfy your personal self. This can't be done no matter what you do. It is a useless attempt of your self seeking to find its Self.

"Searching for the spiritual Self is like 'looking for heaven on earth.' This is impossible because the spiritual Self is what *enlivens* the personal self. It cannot be found *through* the personal self. It can only be reached by *transcending* the personal self.

"Yet, seeking happiness through the personal self is what you strive to do. Everyone around you is trying to do the same thing. You cannot escape the influence of society. But you encounter all sorts of problems with this. You cannot find and hold on to a sense of satisfaction, because of the nature of living on the physical plane.

"At the physical level, things are constantly changing. You find happiness only for a limited time. For example, your body gets tired from too much partying. You get uncomfortably full if you eat too much dessert. You get antsy if you read too much. The body knows its limits, but the desiring mind does not. Experiencing happiness in these ways has to stop or it will turn into pain.

"Because change is a natural part of the physical world, if you achieve something you have desired, it, too, will change. Getting a raise will satisfy you for a while, then you will want another one. Taking a restful vacation will be relaxing at first, then you will become restless and look for something to ease your boredom.

"When you satisfy one desire, another comes in its place. It is like one wave after another continuously breaking against the shore.

"Another problem with desire is that you learn to have new wants by seeing what other people have. The expression 'The grass is always greener on the other side of the street' refers to this. What you already possess doesn't seem to be enough.

"As we have discussed, your mind is used to thinking about one thing after the next. It is like a butterfly going from flower to flower. This is its nature. If you are looking for happiness, your mind will be attracted to one thing it thinks will do the job and make plans for how you can achieve it. Once the desire is attained, your mind will look for another desire to think about. It is like an animal foraging for food. It naturally goes on to the next one. It is constantly creating.

"The urge to create is an expression of the total universe. For example, the universe is constantly creating new stars and galaxies. On a smaller scale, volcanoes on our planet create new mountains and land masses from the lava flow. Changing seasons bring new foliage and the spread of ground cover and flowers. What is true in the larger picture is also true in the smaller. Within a human being, creation is constantly taking place within the mind.

"One reason why your mind continually creates new desires is that nothing turns out to be as good in reality as it was in your imagination. Fantasies about how you want your life to be are always perfect. This is why Buddhists refer to desire as a 'soothing friend.' When you imagine your life with your desire attained, it is pleasurable and provides a sense of escape from day-to-day problems. It stays with you as you go about trying to fulfill your desire. You anticipate feeling contented and your life being perfect.

"The reason your mind imagines perfection is the influence of your spiritual Self, which is, in a basic sense, perfect. On the physical plane, however, things are never perfect. There is always disappointment in satisfying a desire. For example, your camping trip is plagued with mosquitoes, or a large house is expensive to keep up.

"When you work toward realizing a desire, you think about how you will enjoy it when you have obtained it. You project yourself into the future, which prevents you from paying attention to the 'here and now.' Quite often the 'here and now' is painful and you enjoy escaping into your fantasies to ease your feelings about the struggles of daily life.

"But this doesn't solve your problems. It only distracts you from them. It also prevents you from enjoying the good things you already have. You don't stop to smell any roses. The beautiful aspects of your life are unnoticed and unappreciated.

"Take the example of career success. To attain the level to which you aspire requires working long hours. This puts a strain on your physical health. You sacrifice time you could have spent with your family.

"After you achieve your goal, you have to continue to work as hard as you previously did to keep up with your job responsibilities. You may also have others competing for your job, so you worry about that.

"In addition, you probably have grown accustomed to the financial rewards of your position and your lifestyle has changed accordingly. All of this makes it so you can't slow down. You must work at the same pace, or even harder. It is difficult to sit back and enjoy life. Ever present is the fear you will lose what you have worked so hard to achieve. This adds up to a lot of pain.

"This demonstrates why sages say, 'Pleasure is the seed of pain.' It means trying to find pleasure will bring you pain because of all the steps you have to go through to get what you want. Once you have attained it, you have to repeat the steps to satisfy another desire. This brings you even more pain.

"Sages also say, 'Seeking pleasure, being born in pain, also ends in pain.' This means when pleasure is over, you will feel empty because of its loss.

"The way to end the cycle is to realize the only complete and lasting happiness is from your spiritual Self. This is where true happiness resides. It comes from within.

"Buddhists would say trying to find happiness outside yourself by fulfilling desires is like looking to others for your own hands and feet. They are right there within your grasp.

"This doesn't mean you can't participate in life's pleasures, however. It is natural and good to love life. It means you need to understand the nature of happiness at the physical level. It is temporary, a struggle to achieve, and less than perfect.

"If you think it is the only goal in life, you will become lost in the search for it. If you give it its true perspective, you will maintain a detachment from it and accept whatever happens as being okay. This makes room for the influence of your spiritual Self. You can live in the 'Now.' You notice more rainbows and appreciate what you already have, such as a loving family or your physical health. You get a glimpse into the peace and serenity that is at your very core. This is true happiness.

"In the whole scheme of life, desire has a purpose. It provides the impulse necessary to maintain life. It is essential for your development and evolution. Desire acts as a catalyst for you to pursue goals for yourself.

"For example, you learn how to be a better parent through classes and reading. This develops your knowledge. You learn a trade so you can make money and provide a comfortable home for your family. This develops your intellect. You widen the scope of your business to be more productive and sought after. This develops your power. Ambition is necessary in life. Without a personal motive, life would have no meaning. There would be no incentive to work for things.

"Desire leads to experience, out of which grows discrimination, judgment, and self-knowledge. For example, as you work to attain your desires, you learn to be discriminating about which desires are worth the effort necessary to satisfy them. You gain experience in determining what is important to you. You develop your wisdom so that you can see the temporary nature of seeking happiness on the physical level.

"All you need to do is watch yourself as you encounter your desires. Recognize that they are part of your world, as are trees and clouds. You cannot suppress or ignore them. It is only through the experience of being caught up in fulfilling them that you learn how important they should be.

"William Blake said, 'The road to excess leads to the palace of wisdom.' Wisdom frees you from your desires. You learn to let them come and go like clouds in the sky."

NOTES

1. Matthew Fox, *Meditations with Meister Eckhart* (Santa Fe, New Mexico: Bear & Company, Inc., 1982), p. 102.
2. Ken Keyes, Jr., *The Hundredth Monkey* (Coos Bay, Oregon: Love Line Books, 1982).
3. Annie Besant, *A Study in Consciousness* (Madras, India: Theosophical Publishing House, 1938), pp. 276–77.

Self-Realization

YOUR SPIRITUAL PATH

"What does it mean when someone talks about a spiritual path?" Lisa asked.

"Good question," I said. "I know this can be unclear. It can sound as though only those people who have devoted themselves to meditation or religious pursuits are on a spiritual path. But everyone is on a spiritual path. Essentially, it is your personal life.

"Everything you do affects your spiritual development. You may not consciously be trying to improve yourself, but over time it happens. Each experience you go through gives you knowledge and understanding, even if in just a subtle way. The things that don't turn out well, you don't want to repeat. They may happen again, but you gradually learn what works and what doesn't. As time goes by, you evolve a more thorough awareness of yourself and others. You learn simply by living."

"Isn't a spiritual path a set of religious practices a person participates in?" Jane asked.

"It can be," I answered. "It also can be a lifestyle that emphasizes discovering and pursuing a union with your spiritual Self. It may involve prayer, meditation, solitude, and study. The various religions of the world all have practices that are used for spiritual development. I'm sure you all have heard of monks and nuns joining a monastery or convent and devoting themselves to God. Every culture in the world has its own form of this."

"How does someone's everyday life cause him to develop and be closer to God?" asked Jim.

"The God-like qualities a monk or nun strives to perfect are the same qualities you want to express when you relate to others," I said. "Qualities such as patience and kindness are expressions of your spiritual Self. You can work at developing them in your relationships at home, which is a perfect setting for practice.

"Each person makes his own unique 'path' or way in life. Each temperament has a path, or lifestyle, which suits it best. Just as there are a myriad of snowflakes, there are as many paths as there are people.

"Nuns and monks find that a secluded environment works best for them. For others, such as yourselves, a family environment is the best lifestyle from which you can learn.

"A spiritual path is the path toward realizing your Self. You can tread it anywhere. You can learn to express the qualities of your spiritual Self in any setting. This is Self-realization. It is said when you tread the path, you become the path itself."

"So, how do you become Self-realized?" Lisa queried.

"That is just what I was going to present in this evening's class," I said.

"To be Self-realized is to fully know and realize who you are. You know you are the being behind what you do in your day-to-day life. You understand the being is within you all the time. It is what lights you up when you are happy and enjoying life. Its love flows out of you when you are helping others.

"Your spiritual Self is within you even when you are sad and depressed. At those times, because you are immersed in the concerns of your personal self, the influence of your spiritual Self is reduced to a considerable extent, but it is not completely gone.

"It is narrowed due to your narrowed view of yourself. You are conscious only of your sadness and depression. Your sense of self shrinks and becomes limited so that you cannot see the larger picture.

"To counteract this, you place your focus in the opposite direction. You widen your sense of self through a technique called 'witnessing.' "

WITNESSING

"Witnessing is simply stepping back and observing. You watch yourself think your thoughts and feel your feelings. You notice what you do with your body. You witness yourself move from place to place. You become aware of the entire situation. You take it all in because you have enlarged your view of yourself. This is the same as enlarging your consciousness.

"Another word for witnessing is 'mindfulness.' Being mindful of something means giving it your full attention. In witnessing, your mind becomes full of the awareness of everything.

"If you become distracted and get wrapped up in one thing in particular, you lose your awareness of the entire picture. As soon as you catch yourself doing this, you can go back to witnessing once again and watch what is happening.

"Let me give you an example of mindfulness. Think of a mother watching her toddler at a park. She has to pay attention so her child doesn't wander away. She makes sure he doesn't pick up things from the ground and put them in his mouth. The mother can have a conversation with someone, but nevertheless, she is always mindful of what her child is doing."

"So, being mindful is just watching yourself and what is going on?" Jim asked.

"Yes, it is really very simple," I said. "The problem is that you can only do it for a short time. Then you get caught up again with your feelings and thoughts."

"Does being mindful make your life change in any way?" Jane asked.

"Mindfulness, or witnessing, gives you a different perspective on your life," I explained. "You come to see that you are more than your thoughts and actions. You discover that you are the *thinker* of your thoughts and the *doer* of your actions. This brings a new awareness. Soon you realize you are the awareness itself."

"Can it help you when you are depressed?" Lisa inquired.

"It can, because of the change of perspective," I said. "It enables you to no longer identify yourself as the one who is sad and depressed. You identify yourself as the one who is viewing yourself feeling sad and depressed. You realize you are part of something bigger. This is your spiritual Self, illuminating what you see.

"When life's stresses bring you down, you are in a different mode of consciousness than the level of the witness. In witnessing, all is quiet. You are unaffected by a troubled mind and confused emotions.

"For example, witnessing can be a refuge when you are caught up in fear. Rarely is there a concrete reason to fear for your physical safety. More often, you fear someone's disapproval or anger.

"As you witness and watch yourself feel fear, a new strength is found. Fear no longer consumes you. Anger may still come at you, but you can step out of its way. You don't have to react to it with conditioned patterns of behavior or defensiveness. Anger will be like a sword cutting through air. If you give it nothing to oppose, it will disappear by itself."

Al commented, "I have heard the best thing to do when someone gets angry is to be like a mirror. You just stay neutral and don't react. That way, the one who is angry can realize how he is behaving."

"Yes," I said. "This prevents you from a 'knee-jerk' reaction of retaliation. You know from experience if you get mad back, it doesn't accomplish anything. It may blow off some steam, but you will probably find yourself apologizing for your behavior."

"Why should you apologize if you weren't the one who started the fight?" Don asked.

Don's wife, Laura, laughed and shook her head. "That's what I have been going around and around with you about ever since we were first married. I feel we should both say we are sorry when we get into a fight. Even if you weren't necessarily the cause of it, you still contribute to it by raising your voice or getting into a huff!"

"I know you feel that way," Don retorted. Then he softened, and added, "I have been better lately, haven't I? I'm *trying*."

"Yes, you are," Laura conceded.

"What Don and Laura just described are habitual ways two people can respond to one another," I said. "Witnessing dilutes the power of habits. If you simply watch your reactions without justifying them, they start to change.

"This is a type of alchemy or magic. As a child, you may have heard stories about alchemy in which a magician turns lead into gold. Witnessing accomplishes its own form of spiritual alchemy. It heals your emotional wounds with the 'magic' of your spiritual Self."

"Are you just supposed to not react to things that come up?" Jane inquired.

"In a certain way, you don't react," I said. "You still take care of the matter at hand, but your feelings remain quiet."

"How does this happen?" Jane asked.

"It happens slowly," I answered. "Let me explain. As you witness your emotions, you see your own weaknesses. By just watching, these become apparent to you. You analyze what happened to bring them out. You begin to see the inner workings of your defenses and why they get stimulated.

"The unconscious dissolves when brought into consciousness. As you become aware of your automatic defensive reactions, you begin to understand what activates them.

"Initially, you may find yourself silent and not reacting. This is good. It is the first step of change. You may try different ways of handling things or just go through the motions of dealing with matters in an automatic fashion. The important thing is that you maintain your watchfulness, or witnessing.

"As you try different responses, you start to see what ways are better than others to interact in the world. Gradually, you develop the ability to decide what you want to think and feel. You may have a variety of feelings come over you. You decide which feelings you want to keep. Witnessing brings a sense of control that enables this."

Jim sought clarification. "How does witnessing help you control your emotions? It's hard to believe that anything can stop emotions from coming up."

"Witnessing detaches you from your investment in the outcome of whatever you are involved in," I explained. "It allows you to use your intelligence and reason something through. You see yourself and others in a new light. By this kind of analysis, you understand why some of the things you do are ineffective.

"The ancient verses of Hinduism, the Upanishads, have a saying that describes the witness.

> "Two birds, united always and known by the same name,
> "closely cling to the same tree.
> "One of them eats the sweet fruits;
> "the other looks on without eating.[1]

"The bird eating the sweet and sour fruits of life is your personal self. It experiences the highs and lows of your emotions. The other bird, who looks on without eating, is the witness. This symbolizes the detachment of your spiritual Self.

"When you view the world through the eyes of the witness, you see things for what they are. When you forget and go back to interacting through your personality, you are in the grip of the mood of the moment.

"This is what you do most of the time, which is normal. But it isn't a complete picture. It is like a movie screen. The movie seems real, but it is only an illusion of reality. It is just light projected on a screen. When you step back and see the movie screen as well as the projector, you realize you were caught up in the illusion that the movie was real.

"Likewise, when you are going about your life, you believe your thoughts and feelings are real. They are, but only in a limited sense. This is your personal self. Its point of view is very restricted. When you step back and witness yourself feeling your emotions, you see that you are more than your personal self. You see that you are the spirit behind it all.

"The world in which the personal self interacts is the illusion. The real world is that of the being who watches what is happening.

"When you witness, you see the world as a delightful show. You enjoy it while it lasts and forget about it when it is over. Your consciousness remains detached and observing. It is like watching the customs of people in a foreign country. You sit back and look on without getting involved.

"This same is true with everything that happens in your life. From the point of view of the witness, you aren't attached to how the events in your life proceed. You just let them unfold.

"Sue, a few sessions ago you described what it means to center yourself. Is this the same thing?" Al asked.

CENTERING YOURSELF

"Yes, 'centering' yourself is witnessing," I said. "To center yourself, you step back from the situation you find yourself in. You relax, pause, and clear your mind. It is helpful to do this when you are under stress. Then you can act with more wisdom.

"This is what it is meant by the expression 'to collect yourself.' You are actually 'collecting' your spiritual Self and using it to help you.

"The witness is an unidentified being. There is no sense of being this or that. It looks through the vehicle of the mind, yet it is not the mind. It is an *opening* in the mind."

To illustrate this, I picked up a piece of notebook paper and pointed to a hole in the margin. "It is like the hole in this piece of paper. It is still considered paper, yet the hole is not *of* paper.

"The witness is the same. It is considered part of you, sitting there in your flesh and bones. Yet, it is like the hole in the paper. It is not composed of flesh and bones. It is an opening, through which your mind can be flooded with light.

"The witness is not the light. The light is your spiritual Self. The light enables and enlightens the witness. It is the force behind it."

Lisa spoke up. "When I think about the witness in me, as you are describing it in your talk, I am aware of how quiet it is."

"That is true. A characteristic of witnessing is the experience of silence at a very deep level. There may be sounds in your environment, but the silence is at the level of your spiritual Self. It is the backdrop for everything.

"The seventeenth-century Japanese poet, Matsuo Basho, wrote:

"The temple bell stops
"But I still hear the sound
"Coming out of the flowers.

"This is a poetic way of describing the sound of the witness, which is the sound of silence.

"When you witness, your rise above your thoughts as you would rise in an airplane, which allows you to see all the people, buildings, and workings of a city as one. By not focusing on anything in particular, you are able to watch with this kind of perspective.

"When you are witnessing, you withdraw from the experience. Your mind is in abeyance. As this deepens, the 'I am me' dissolves. You move into the sense of 'I am all.'

"Meister Eckhart described this when he said, 'The eye with which I see God is the same eye with which God sees me.'[2] Witnessing is a discovery of the eye seeing itself, or the eye seeing its Self."

"Can you witness and still go about your day-to-day life?" asked Al.

"Yes, the witness is available for you to reach at any time," I said. "All you need to do is keep it in mind."

"It seems it would be hard to remember to do this, particularly when you get busy," Jane asked.

"At first it is," I said. "You forget about it and only occasionally remember it. But if you practice it often, gradually it becomes second nature.

"Let me give you an analogy to think about. When you are looking for something you have lost, you keep it in your mind until you run across it. The same is true with witnessing. If you keep the witness in mind continuously, it becomes a habit. Then you will always have a bridge to your spiritual Self.

"In the Kabbalah of Judaism, the concept of 'creation taking place every instant' is the same as witnessing. You watch life come into being.

"In the Christian tradition, the equivalent idea is 'walking with Jesus at your side.' It is witnessing the wonder of life.

"Einstein understood this when he said, 'There are only two ways to live your life. One is as though nothing is a miracle. The other is as though everything is a miracle.' This appreciation comes from your spiritual Self. There is an gratefulness for whatever happens. When you witness, you marvel at what unfolds. You enjoy it all because you are one with all.

"I don't mean to be a 'stick in the mud,' " Don complained, "but I just don't get it. I don't understand what you mean by 'the witness.' "

"That's okay, Don," I assured him. "It isn't easy to grasp. Let me give you a practical example."

I held up a cup of water. "One way to experience the witness is to watch yourself take a drink of water or coffee. Don, watch yourself as you do this."

As Don drank from the cup, I continued, "Who is it that determines you need to lift your arm and raise the cup to your lips? Who is it that notices the taste of the coffee?"

"Well, it's me!" Don answered.

"Yes, that is the 'you' I am talking about," I said.

"That's easy," Don smiled. "You mean the witness is just me?"

"Yes, it is the 'you' who watches yourself go through the actions to drink from a cup or do anything," I explained. "It is your awareness.

"What about the rest of the class? Try it yourselves and see what you discover."

The members of the class each took a drink. Jane spoke up. "I see what you mean. It is my being aware of drinking from my cup that is the witness, right?"

"Yes, that's it," I said. "There is a sense of detachment from the process. You feel like you are standing back and merely observing. There is a bit of unreality to it, as if you are in suspension and not really in the world. Do you understand what I mean?"

"Yes, I do," said Jane.

Jim said, "I think I do, too. But I'm not sure if I understand what you mean about there being no more 'I.' I realize the 'I' is the personal self. But it seems that 'I' still exist when I am witnessing."

"It does. But it is a different 'I.' The 'I' used to be you in your personal self. With the witness, the 'I' expands and becomes the link between your personal self and your spiritual Self.

"The witness doesn't need to identify itself as anything because it is pure consciousness. It doesn't need to think of itself as 'I am this' or 'I am that.' It is more than a list of your personal characteristics.

"Let me give you another example. When you are watching your dreams while sleeping, you don't refer to yourself as 'I.' You just watch. It is the same witness. The dream can feel real, just as your life in the physical world can seem real. But it is just like the picture on the movie screen. It is an illusion of reality. What is real is the witness."

"That is such a good example," Lisa said enthusiastically. "When I think about watching my dreams, it is very clear I am not in the dream. The 'I' is detached and removed from my actions. So, 'I' as a being am watching the dream. Is that my spiritual Self?"

"Yes," I said. "It is the connection to your spiritual Self."

"But life seems so real. Why is that?" asked Jane.

"It only seems real because you are immersed in it," I answered. "It is 'real' on its own level, but it is limited and constantly changing. The point I'm trying to make is that your consciousness doesn't have to get consumed by the events on the physical plane. It can learn to exist from the standpoint of the witness, as well. This is your spiritual Self.

"When you look out at the world from the eyes of the witness, you sense that your awareness is all-encompassing. It seems as broad as the sky, yet bigger than the sky. There is no beginning nor end. It envelops the entire landscape and everything in it. It encompasses your thoughts, feelings, and actions. This is the meaning of the saying 'Everything is in you.' The 'you' is the opening to your awareness. It is your true Self. Realizing this is Self-realization."

SELF-REALIZATION

"The Self, or your awareness, does not move from place to place. The world moves in it. The essence of who you are does not change. It just looks like a departure from place to place. You are here, there, and everywhere."

"This seems so easy," Lisa said.

"It really is," I responded. "Again, the difficult part is to remember it. At first, it is hard to remain in this state for long. The mind and the emotions can be very persuasive in their ability to make you think that you want what they want.

"But you are the awareness behind your thinking and feeling. You are what watches this entire process. You are in the driver's seat. You have the power to think and feel whatever you want, or not to think or feel anything.

"If you practice watching yourself without reacting right away, you develop the ability to choose how you will respond. You understand that your immediate reactions are only to be used as information for you to analyze. They are guideposts that tell you things you need to know about life on the physical plane.

"As you grow into this awareness, you see that the body, the emotions, and the mind work spontaneously. You don't have to do anything. You can relax and just be. After all, you are a human *being*, not a human *doing*.

"Becoming Self-realized is not an experience you try to have. Neither is it a prescribed way of living your life. It is a way of looking at your life. It is an attitude more than anything else. A Buddhist metaphor says, 'Words are only fingers pointing at the moon. If you look at the fingers, you can't see the moon.' *Trying* to be Self-realized will get in your way. It will be like glue and hold you back. The only effort you make is when you shift your attention. It is really just a letting go and a watching. This is the witness.

"You may hear about 'connecting' to your spiritual Self. In reality, you don't connect or unite to your spiritual Self. You simply realize it is there, and has been all the time.

"What you thought was you — the personal self — is not divided from the spiritual part of you at all. It only seems that way until you develop a fuller realization of your true nature. This 'dawns' on you from the light of the spiritual Self."

I took out a box and opened it on the table in front of the class. "I have some common items from the hardware store that demonstrate the various degrees of understanding you go through as the awareness of your spiritual Self gradually unfolds."

I picked up a twelve-inch-square mirror. Holding it up and looking into it, I said, "This mirror represents the barrier your consciousness has when it is immersed in the life of your personal self. All you see is yourself. You identify with what you see in the mirror. It consumes you. It is impossible to see through it to look at things from the 'eyes' of your spiritual Self."

Next, I picked up a piece of translucent plastic. It was cloudy white, allowing light to pass through. I asked the class what they thought the degree of openness to the spiritual Self would be if the plastic was the personal self.

Lisa answered, "I think that would be similar to someone first learning to meditate. He may not be able to perceive much of his spiritual Self, but he wouldn't be as preoccupied with himself."

Al said, "I agree. He would be able to perceive a little bit of the light of the spiritual Self, the way the plastic allows some light to come through. I wouldn't think he would have much clarity, though."

"Good thinking," I said. "What about this next item?"

I picked up a piece of glass and held it up to my face. "What is this like?"

"That must be similar to a devout monk or nun praying or meditating," Lisa said.

Al suggested, "Is it what Jesus Christ was like as He lived in the world? The Bible says He was God made incarnate in man. The glass would be the same as His body. Since it is 'see-through,' it represents His personal self, which lets the light of His spiritual Self shine through perfectly."

"That's very insightful, Al," I said. "What about if there was nothing in the way of your consciousness functioning fully in your personal self and your spiritual Self?"

Jane noted, "I think if there is no barrier between your consciousness and God, you must be in 'heaven.' "

"Or," Jim suggested, "what about when Jesus was performing his miracles? It seems he must have been one with God at those times."

"I like that idea, Jim," Lisa said.

Don's frustration was apparent when he said, "I can't imagine what any of this would be like. I must have something like a piece of concrete in front of my eyes."

"Don't be so hard on yourself, Don," Lisa reassured him. "You're not that bad."

"I agree. Don't get discouraged," I said. "You will eventually be able to open up to your spiritual Self, if not through meditation then through other efforts."

Perplexed, Don asked, "What good does this all do? What is the point of being Self-realized?"

"In a nutshell, Self-realization makes you a better person," I said. "It comes from a natural urge within you. Just like you want to do well on a test or running a race, you also want to be the best person you can be in life.

"When you first hear about Self-realization, you may want to attain it because of the desire to achieve something or to feel special. This is natural in the process of your evolution. Soon that fades and you feel the desire for Self-realization as a pull from within. That pull comes from your spiritual Self."

"What does it mean when you hear about Self-realization being a mystical experience?' Lisa asked.

"The word 'mystical' refers to something that is beyond the range of ordinary knowledge," I said. "It refers to mysterious experiences that are incomprehensible and only understood by intuition. Mystical refers to your spiritual nature.

"Almost everyone can relate to mystical experiences. They can happen spontaneously or at a particular place, such as a holy site. You may experience the oneness of nature as you spend time outdoors. You are aware of something much greater than yourself.

"These experiences may happen only a few times in your life. In between, you might hear only faint 'whisperings' from your spiritual Self, if that. But, by witnessing, you remind yourself that you are a spiritual being. It helps you remain open to the mystical part of yourself.

"St. Paul in Philippians 4:7 refers to the mystical and unfathomable nature of your spiritual Self when he describes Self-realization as 'the peace of God which passeth all understanding.' It is something you cannot discern with your everyday mind. It is beyond normal comprehension."

"It is hard to hold on to the awareness. As I try to do it while you are talking, it keeps fading," Lisa said.

"I know what that's like," I agreed. "It takes practice to keep the awareness of your Self in mind. Meister Eckhart spoke of this when he wrote, 'God is at home. It is we who have gone out for a walk.'[3] Returning to the state of witnessing brings you back 'home' to your Self.

"Don't get discouraged if it seems as though you're not getting anywhere. Just take it a little at a time. Each time you step back and witness, you strengthen that ability.

"Remember, a ten-mile hike is accomplished by taking one step at a time, one after another. Each individual step may not seem important, but it is. The hike may seem endless until you reach the end, but you eventually do. The same is true with Self-realization. Every effort brings you closer to your goal.

"When you get bogged down with the stresses of life, you feel alone and apart from your Self. This is only temporary. In time, you will be at one with your Self once again. It is like the Hindu metaphor that says the wave grieves over its separation from the ocean. Yet, when its grief subsides, it realizes it is the Ocean.

"The same is true for you. Witnessing helps you realize your spiritual Self.

"Self-realization will happen for everyone. No one ever fails. It is represented in the expression my grandmother used to say, 'Seeds must be there for the plant to grow.'

"The 'seed' of spiritual awakening is within everyone. Just as a seed grows in silence and in darkness until it is ready to sprout, the awareness of your spiritual Self is enmeshed in the darkness of your personal self until it is ripe for realization. The seed will eventually sprout. The same is true with you. You will eventually become aware of your Self.

"Another Hindu metaphor states this beautifully. Like the beautiful water lily grows up from the mud, as you rise above identifying with your personal self, you can realize your Self.

"Mabel Collins, in her inspired book *Light on the Path*, refers to Self-realization as a flower that 'blooms in the silence that follows the storm.'[4] The storm is your being caught up in the stressful events of your life. Storms of anger and confusion arise again and again. They are like the recurring storms of nature.

"The opening of the bloom is when you first perceive the awareness of your true being. You pause in the wonder of it. Then you experience the silence. With it comes the realization of bliss.

"Teachers say you must spend a lot of time experiencing life from the point of view of your personal self before you become aware that there is something more. Just as dawn comes slowly, you gradually realize the true essence of your spiritual nature.

"This is the great mystery of life. You are constantly seeking your spiritual Self, yet it is there all along. It is a paradox, a contradiction.

"A story from Africa illustrates this struggle.[5] A hunter, unable to find game, pleads with the Chief Priest of the Forest to help him. The priest complies and gives the hunter six pumpkin seeds. The hunter, seeking fast wealth, hopes the seeds are magical and puts them in his horse pack.

"When he returns home, he is disappointed to find that they are still seeds. In frustration, he gives them to the first person he meets. This happens to be a farmer, who plants the seeds, raises an abundant crop, and sells it at the market. Over time, he becomes quite wealthy.

"The hunter goes back into the forest to tell the priest that the seeds are no good, but he never finds him again. The moral is 'What you are searching for is what you already have.'

"The Chinese philosopher Hui-neng/Daikan said, 'As far as Buddha nature [the spiritual Self] is concerned, there is no difference between an enlightened man and an ignorant one. What makes the difference is that one realizes it, while the other is kept in ignorance of it.'

"The spiritual Self does not change after Self-realization. It is the same whether you perceive it or not. It is an unchanging presence. What changes is the unfolding of your awareness about it.

"The necessity of living in the world through your body and personality also doesn't change when you realize your Self. You still go about your life, doing whatever is necessary to survive. The only difference is that you know your spiritual Self intimately and deeply. It is constantly in mind.

"A Zen Buddhist poem illustrates this.

> "Before Enlightenment, chop wood, carry water.
> "After Enlightenment, chop wood, carry water.

"You need to cook dinner and earn a living, even if you are Self-realized.

"Another Zen story by Ch'ing-yuan/Seigen portrays the same process.

> "Before I came to Zen, mountains were only mountains,
> rivers only rivers, and trees were only trees. After I got

into Zen, mountains were no longer mountains, rivers were no longer rivers, and trees were no longer trees. When Enlightenment happened, mountains again were only mountains, rivers again only rivers, and trees again were only trees.

"At first, you see the beauty in the environment and the natural wonders of the earth. There is a newfound joy. You feel one with nature.

"Eventually, you realize the serenity is within you and has been there all the time. When you realize your true Self, the importance of experiencing nature is not necessary. You know you can feel the tranquillity anytime and anywhere you want."

"Are psychics Self-realized?" Lisa asked.

"People who are clairvoyant may or may not be," I said. "It depends upon the nature of their abilities. They are able to perceive things beyond the normal range of the senses, such as seeing auras or knowing someone's feelings. They may be able to see a person's past, predict the future, and possibly comprehend past lives. The ability of a clairvoyant is largely determined by the degree of development of his or her intuition.

"However, it is important to remember the capability of a clairvoyant doesn't necessarily mean the person is spiritual. People who can see auras often understand the Oneness of all life. But this is not necessarily true for everyone with psychic skills.

"Everybody has some degree of psychic ability, although some have more sensitivity than others. The key is living it. It is acting in a way that is in harmony with the Unity of all. A spiritual person understands this and tries to radiate the qualities of the spiritual Self, such as kindness and acceptance."

"If you become Self-realized, do you become clairvoyant?" asked Lisa.

"No, that isn't necessarily true, either," I said. "You will continue to develop an understanding of yourself and others, though. It is natural for this to improve.

"You won't automatically see auras. That isn't the goal. Seeing auras doesn't do much good anyway, unless you have developed empathy with others to understand what the colors of the aura mean. By the way, there is a down side to being psychic or clairvoyant. You become more sensitive to negative energy, also.

"Let me tell you a story which illustrates this. A clairvoyant friend and I visited a beautiful church that was about one hundred years old. It had impressive architecture with high ceilings and stained glass windows depicting the glory of God and the heavens.

"When we entered the church, my friend was affected greatly by the energy of the sanctuary which was filled with years and years of people's grief, desperation, and emotional upset. She picked all this up. I couldn't. All I saw was the grandness of the architecture.

"A certain lack of sensitivity to the energy of others is nature's protection. There is a lot of good energy in the world, but also a lot of negativity. To be sensitive is a double-edged sword. It isn't the goal. The goal is to discover your true nature and live in harmony with your spiritual Self. If you do this, you will be following the Buddhist teaching that directs you to 'go to the root, don't worry about the branches.'

"This guides you to express the qualities of your spiritual Self as you live in the world, rather than worrying about the benefits for yourself."

Lisa asked, "If you work at developing the awareness of your spiritual Self through witnessing, what kind of changes happen in how you live your life?"

SURRENDER

"Probably the biggest influence of witnessing is that it enables you to develop an acceptance of whatever happens in your life. You abandon your need to control things. You relinquish the wants of your personal self. You let go of your desires. However, you still go about the business of living. You do your work and participate in activities, but you aren't as personally involved with how things turn out. This is what is means to surrender. It is a quality of the state of witnessing.

"You know what surrender is because you do it when you fall asleep. When you are lying in bed waiting to doze off, you make no conscious effort for sleep to come. You surrender to it. You give up all control and glide into sleep.

"This is described in Chinese as 'wei wu wei,' which means 'doing not doing,' or doing nothing. This is non-action and non-interference in the natural course of events in your life. It is letting go and allowing whatever is going on to happen.

"If you try to be Self-realized, it interferes with the 'letting-go' process necessary for witnessing. Surrender means to settle back, relax, open yourself up, and allow events to unfold at their own pace.

"Don't aim toward the goal of Self-realization. It will happen by itself. It is summed up in the saying from the Chinese teacher Lao-Tzu in the *Tao Te Ching*, 'If you want to become full, you must let yourself be empty.'⁶ You empty yourself of desire and the investment in how you want your life to be.

"In surrender, you trust the way your life is going. You trust the intelligence of the universe, just as a dancer trusts the intelligence of her body. The dancer relaxes her conscious will and becomes one with the dance. So, too, you become one with the flow of life. It is a natural process.

"Surrender allows you to have a quiet mind. When your mind is quiet, you have a sense of emptiness and nothingness. This is the space into which the spiritual Self can expand.

"Several metaphors from Lao-Tzu speak to this. Spokes join together in a wheel, but it is the center hole that makes it spin. Straw is woven into a basket, but the emptiness inside holds its contents. Bricks and wood make a house, but you use the empty space inside to live.

"Lao-Tzu said the tangible has its purpose, but the intangible is what you use. The same is true with your mind. It works to help you live in the world, but you use an empty and still mind to open to your spiritual Self."

I took off a scarf I was wearing around my neck and gripped it firmly in one hand. "If I hold on to this scarf too tightly, I cannot feel it." I loosened my hold on the scarf and pulled it with my other hand. "Only by letting it slip through my fingers can I feel it.

"The same is true with your life. Only by letting go can you experience it.

"Lao-Tzu gives a few more examples of surrender. You have probably heard it said that a good traveler is not intent upon arriving, but enjoys wherever he is. Likewise, a good artist lets his creativity lead him wherever it wants. A good scientist frees herself from preconceived concepts and keeps her mind open to new discoveries.

"Just like a plant grows on its own, let events take their course. Picking a fruit too soon will ruin what is almost ripe. Rushing into something can cause you to fail. Trying to grasp things will cause you to lose them. This is true if you try to hold on to someone's love for you. If you become possessive, you lose the awareness of the love in the present.

"Spiritual teachers say to live as the flower grows, which unconsciously opens itself to the sun. A rose is inherently beautiful. The same is true with you.

"Wise advice given to someone who wants to impress a first date is 'be yourself.' This instructs you to be natural and unaffected. You relax and realize that if a relationship is going to start, it will, whether you do anything in particular or not."

Lisa volunteered, "I think this is important to remember when I worry about how I look. I realize people aren't going to like me any more or less because of what I am wearing or how my hair looks that day."

"So true," I said. "Trying to be someone other than who you are is bound to fail. As the *Tao Te Ching* says, 'One on tiptoe cannot stand. One who displays himself does not shine. He dims his own light. He who defines himself cannot know who he really is. He who has power over others cannot empower himself. He who clings to his work will create nothing that endures.'⁷ This says you can accomplish more in life if you remove your personal attachment from the outcome of your efforts.

"Surrender takes place when someone who is devoted to God turns over his problems to Him. The weight of the problems lessens. You accept whatever happens as 'God's will.'

"It is the same as asking the Holy Spirit to come into your life. This nurtures peacefulness and tranquillity. You may have heard the expression, 'Let come what comes and let go what goes.' This is the same thing."

"Does surrender help in relationships?" Lisa asked.

"Yes, surrender allows you to accept people as they are," I said. "You don't blame them for their faults and failures. You realize they are doing the best they can and you don't judge them.

"It is the same when you injure yourself doing something you are inexperienced at. You don't blame your body. Rather, you nurse yourself back to health. You accept it and help the process of healing. This is surrender.

"Surrender teaches you to give allowances to people in the same way you would to someone you are close to. You aren't really separate from them, anyway. They are all your brothers and sisters because you are all part of the same Unity.

"It is important to remember to apply this to yourself, as well. Restrain from self-criticism when you don't act the way you want. You are still mastering your personal self. Being kind toward yourself will help you be that way to others. Meister Eckhart said, 'Friendly relations with another spring from friendly relations with your self.'[8] This can also be interpreted as meaning you should have a friendly or close relationship with your spiritual Self."

"How can surrender help you if you see someone in your family having a problem?" Jane asked. "It would be hard to sit back and watch without doing something about it."

"Surrender doesn't mean you don't do anything to solve problems," I said. "You still try to find a resolution to situations you are involved in. Remember, you still need to 'chop wood and carry water' after enlightenment. You continue to use your capabilities to try to work things out.

"Surrender means you trust yourself and the process you go through to resolve whatever is happening. You don't set your mind on one particular outcome. You do the best you can and accept whatever happens, whether it is disappointing or what you were hoping for.

"For example, suppose you need to talk to a neighbor who is infringing on you in some way. To surrender to the process means you don't impose your own particular solution on him when you address the problem. You speak from a position of neutrality. You are patient and calm in your demeanor. You allow him to solve the problem he is creating, rather than argue for the solution you think is right.

"If this doesn't work and you need to take other steps, do so with the same equanimity. You may even decide to do nothing. But if you go through the process with the detachment of the witness, you will have a smoother interaction, less stress, and probably a better result.

"The attitude of surrender offers another benefit. If you have been harmed by the actions of another, surrender allows you to let go of your injury and accept the other person despite what he has done. The mystics of Islam, the Sufis, have a saying that expresses this: 'Oh, break my heart. Oh, break it again. So I can learn to love you even more.' "

Jane noted, "That sounds like the unconditional love parents feel as they raise their children. There are countless times a mother or father must accept the behavior of a child and forgive and forget."

"Yes, you're right," I said. "Parents do this throughout the entire process of child-rearing. Surrender is also how parents handle their children's need to grow up and make their own mistakes. Sometimes this is the only way kids learn. Parents know they have to let them go.

"Surrender is what birds do when they are learning to fly. It is said that birds learn by falling. They let go and fly without doubting their ability. Then they are given wings.

"Surrender helps you become aware of the insignificance of things that occur in life. You realize that what you do today has little importance in the whole scheme of things.

"Something may come up that feels like a dire circumstance, but as time goes by, you forget it happened. You learn perspective. You realize what you do in life doesn't really matter. It is the process that is important, or 'how you play the game.' This is the lesson of surrender.

"Hindu philosophy instructs us to be like water. Water is one of the softest and the strongest materials in the world. It fits any container. It may seem weak, but it can penetrate rock. The key word is 'flow.' Flowing with life is surrender.

"When you surrender, you abandon your personal desires and wants in any given situation. You don't have a preconceived agenda about how things should be. As a result, you reduce the amount of karma you make for yourself.

"Because you are not actively seeking anything, you generate no 'cause' which would bring a future result. If something positive happens, you enjoy it. If it doesn't, you aren't disappointed because you weren't invested in a particular result. You have a detachment that lets you simply watch your life reveal itself.

"In Buddhist philosophy, this is implied when it is said, 'A Master's steps don't leave footprints.' The footprints represent the mark you leave in the world. It is the karma from your actions. A Master doesn't make karma because he has no attachments. He doesn't need to leave his mark because he is not trying to accomplish anything for himself.

"An old story about farmer and a horse illustrates this concept. This is how it goes.

"A poor farmer's horse ran off into the country. All his neighbors offered their condolences, but the farmer said, 'How do you know this isn't good fortune?'

"A few months later, the horse came back with several wild horses. The farmer's neighbors all rejoiced over his good fortune.

"The farmer's son was overjoyed and tried to train one of the wild horses. He fell off and broke his leg. Once again, the neighbors offered the farmer their condolences. But the farmer said, 'How do you know this isn't good fortune?'

"Soon after that, the country was invaded and all the able-bodied men were conscripted into the army. The farmer's son couldn't go because of his broken leg. Nine-tenths of the men died in the war. Once again, the neighbors rejoiced over the farmer's good fortune.

"This story illustrates how seemingly unfortunate circumstances can turn out to be for the best. You never know what the future holds. Surrender helps you accept whatever comes along.

"Many times in life when circumstances force you to make an unexpected change, a greater purpose is being served. It may not be apparent at the time, but some aspect of the change will be for the better.

"For example, a student endeavoring to be accepted into a particular school program finds out his application has been turned down. He changes his career aspirations, only to discover that his new field of study is a better choice for him.

"Do any of you have examples like this?"

Don spoke up, "I remember when my parents had to move to a different town when I was growing up. I was devastated. I missed my friends and the school I had attended. Pretty soon I adjusted, though. It turned out my sports ability was appreciated more at the town we moved to because the high school was smaller. I was one of the top players on the football team. This wouldn't have happened at my old school because there were so many more kids to pick from to make a team. I also met my future wife there."

Jim said he was laid off from his first job because of a change in management. He was worried that working only a short time at the company would look bad to future employers. It turned out he found a job right away at a new company where he received better pay and benefits.

Anne described the circumstances in which she and Jim met. She had been stood up by a date, which freed her to accept a blind date her roommate wanted her to go on. The blind date was Jim. She fell in love that first night. She couldn't have been more grateful for being stood up.

"Even though it may not seem positive when you are forced to make a change, something good often comes from it," I said. "The attitude of surrender will help you accept whatever happens."

"Can you be Self-realized and go to work to earn money?" Al asked.

"Yes, being Self-realized doesn't mean you reject responsibilities," I answered. "However, you keep them in their proper perspective. You understand you are not doing it by yourself. It is the influence of your spiritual Self that allows you to create and achieve. If you remember this, you won't identify with what you produce.

"Just as it is natural to breathe, it is natural to work, teach, and create. Spiritual teachers say that you should do your best with your talents because these are gifts from God or the Creator. Do so, however, with the realization that your achievements are possible only through the power of your spiritual Self. Witnessing and surrender can help you remember this."

LIVING IN THE PRESENT

"Another important advantage you gain from surrendering your personal motives is that you are able to be aware of the present.

"You all probably have heard the phrase about living 'in the present.' This means to let go of whatever you are preoccupied with and simply notice what is happening at each moment. While moods vary and activities come and go, your awareness of what is going on at that particular moment doesn't change. You can sense that it is always there. It transcends time. This allows you to perceive the 'Now.'

"To elucidate what it means to live in the present, I'd like to talk a little about time and how it is perceived. The perception of time is produced by your awareness of what is happening from moment to moment.

"The object of your awareness is always changing. One moment, you may be interacting with your children. In another moment, you are doing a chore. There is an unending progression of moments, each appearing out of nothing and disappearing into nothing. They never reappear. Nothing ever remains the same, even for a fraction of a second.

"The sensation of the present comes from one fleeting glimpse of your world. In this momentary glance, your awareness of the present is made possible because of the illumination from your spiritual Self.

"The sense that time has gone by is the result of your memory. Memory is the recollection of several moments together. This gives a sense of the past. The memory stays with you and can be recalled at any time. It causes you to think you will act and feel the same way in the future. You identify yourself with who you were in the past and project that onto events yet to come.

"However, this is all in your mind. It is an illusion. It is caused by your personal self and it's easy to identify with.

"One reason the past and the future are said to be illusions is because they are constantly changing. First of all, your memory changes because you go through different experiences each day that add new information to your memory. You also feel differently about the past as the experiences in your life accumulate. You gain a sense of perspective so that strong feelings change or are forgotten.

"The future isn't any more real than the past. You may look forward to an upcoming event, but the future has yet to arrive. When the event happens, you may be disappointed if it doesn't go as you expected. This is a common occurrence, because nothing ever turns out the way you imagine it will. Because you look into the future from your perspective alone, everything goes your way. This is another example of the way your mind makes a world of illusions.

"Memories are forgotten until you are reminded of them. Then they are brought into the present where they seem to come alive again. But this is still only in the mind. True satisfaction comes only from being aware of who you are in the present moment.

"The present is exceptional and unique. It stands out as if illumined. It has a 'stamp of reality' to it.

"This isn't true of the past or the future. Neither the anticipation of an event nor its memory can equal the event itself. What makes the present different is the presence of your spiritual Self. It enlightens your awareness and makes it real.

"The encouragement to live in the 'Now' is well stated by T.S. Eliot in 'Four Quartets':

> "What might have been and what has been
> "Point to one end, which is always present.

"Living with your awareness in the 'Now' allows you to resolve painful experiences more effectively. If you feel grief over the loss of someone through death or separation, witnessing your feelings lessens the degree that they consume you. The hold your grief has over you is reduced.

"When you have been close to someone and he or she is no longer in your life, it is natural to feel an emptiness. You, as a human being, are a creature of habit. You miss what you were accustomed to doing with your loved one. By watching yourself, however, you open the door for the painful feelings to recede more quickly. You stop ruminating about the past and allow new habits to develop and replace the old ones.

"When you are upset emotionally, it is particularly important to live in the 'Now.' Otherwise, you tend to re-enact events in your mind, recalling pain and other troubling memories. This keeps you living in the past.

"The cultures of Polynesia and Hawaii have a concept called 'manawa.'[9] It is translated as 'Now is the moment of power.' This means that the only time you can use your power is in the present moment.

"In the past, you have no power. You cannot change it. Neither do you have power over the future. It is yet to come. The most important time is the present, when you choose how you want your life to be.

"Our fast-paced society gives a sense of urgency to everything that happens. People feel they don't have enough time to do all they need to do, let alone have time for relaxation. My grandmother used to say, 'Rushing from one thing to another doesn't add time to your life.'

"Living in the present is the way to make the most out of the time you have. When you are with your children, you can fully appreciate them, rather than hurry them through their homework or household chores.

"If you feel overwhelmed by all your responsibilities and obligations, you might find it helpful to simplify your life, picking and choosing what is important and what can be eliminated. If you don't stop to 'smell the roses along the way,' you will miss them. A rainbow is out for only a few minutes. What you are trying to accomplish can wait while you appreciate it.

"Sören Kierkegaard said, 'Most men pursue pleasure with such breathless haste they hurry past it.' When you are caught up in the pursuit of something, you can't enjoy the good things you have right now.

"In conclusion, because the 'past is history and the future is a mystery,' the only thing to do is appreciate the present. Some say it is a gift, or a present, from God.

"Well, we have had a thorough and stimulating discussion tonight. Your questions have been probing and deep. Let us close for the evening with a brief meditation.

"Relax, get into a comfortable position, and close your eyes.

"Let us feel harmony with the group.

"Let us feel harmony with nature, picturing a tree with its roots deep into the ground."

"Be aware of the present moment. Forget all your concerns of the day and just be aware of the 'Now.'

"Let your awareness recede deep within yourself. Allow it to expand into the cave of your heart.

"Experience the peace and silence that is at the core of your being.

"Lastly, picture yourself going through your week with this new awareness. See yourself as the witness, watching yourself participate in your activities. Be aware of the sense of detachment. Allow that to continue to grow and develop, knowing the peace and serenity you feel now is yours whenever you want."

NOTES

1. Swami Nikhilananda, *Upanishads*, Vol. II (New York: Ramakrishna-Vivekananda Center, 1952), p. 134.
2. Matthew Fox, *Meditations with Meister Eckhart* (Santa Fe, New Mexico: Bear & Company, Inc., 1982), p. 21.
3. Ibid., p. 15.
4. Mabel Collins, *Light on the Path* (Madras, India: The Theosophical Publishing House, 1911), p. 37.
5. Awo Fa'lokun Fatunmbi, *Iba'se Orisa* (New York: Original Publications, 1994), p. 69.
6. Lao-Tzu, *Tao Te Ching*, Stephen Mitchell, trans. (New York: Harper Collins, 1988), p. 22.
7. Ibid., p. 24.
8. Fox, *Meditations with Meister Eckhart*, p. 105.
9. Serge King, *Kahuna Healing* (Wheaton, Illinois: Theosophical Publishing House, 1983), pp. 128–29.

The Field of Unity

"I'd like to start this session with a brief meditation influenced by one of the Buddhist traditions. It is a common practice to open a Buddhist teaching with a short prayer or meditation called 'Adjusting the Motivation.'

"All of you probably were motivated to take this class to learn something for your growth. That is good. But a dedicated Buddhist widens that motivation to include a more altruistic desire. He or she wishes not only to gain knowledge to become a better person, but also to achieve enlightenment in order to serve all other sentient or living beings.

"As you adjust your motivation in preparation for this class, strive to learn the principles of spirituality so you may use them to benefit others. It doesn't matter how you do this. It may be in the smallest of ways. That is fine. Your inner motivation is the key.

"Let us relax and allow a feeling of harmony to come into our hearts. Extend the feelings of good will to the surrounding community.

"In conclusion, let us be aware of the greater purpose for this class as we strive to apply what we are learning in order to assist others."

LEVELS OF CONSCIOUSNESS

Personal Self   Physical Body and Body Mind

                  Emotional Body

                  Lower Mental Body — *This is the everyday mind.*

Spiritual Self   Higher Mental Body — *This is the part of the*
                        mind that receives intuition and utilizes reason
                        and wisdom.

                  Intuitional Body

                  Field of Unity

"Tonight, we will be discussing the Field of Unity. As you can see on the chart, it is the highest level of consciousness.

"The Field of Unity can also be called the Field of Love. This is the plane of consciousness where the spiritual essence of everything in the universe coalesces as one. In this dimension, nothing separates the spiritual nature of one thing and another. All is united as a whole.

"Out of Unity, humanity emerges on the physical plane. Yet there is an aspect of the plane of Unity in everyone and everything. Just as a bee gathers nectar from all flowers, at the heart of each individual is the same spiritual essence. Each is still of the One, but separate in physical form and personality.

"Arising from the field of Unity comes an infinite number of expressions on the physical plane. This is what makes each person unique. No two are alike. It is like the clouds in the sky. Each cloud has its own shape, yet each is of the same substance.

"It is said that only by seeing all the clouds together can you perceive heaven. The same is true with humanity. Seeing it as a whole helps you grasp the Unity within.

"The individuality found in each person parallels what is seen in nature. For example, variations of color and form make each flower unique. If you look at a whole hillside of flowers, however, the diversity within becomes hidden. You see all the flowers as a whole.

"Alfred, Lord Tennyson, the English poet, wrote a poem about the difficulty in comprehending the nature of the plane of Unity:

"Flower in the crannied wall,

"I pluck you out of the crannies,

"I hold you here, root and all, in my hand,

"Little flower — but if I could understand

"What you are, root and all, and all in all,

"I should know what God and man is.

"You may have seen a popular lamp on the market these days called a 'lava lamp.' Lava lamps demonstrate how each individual comes from and returns back to the same spiritual source.

"A lava lamp is a decorative lamp composed of a light shining through a thick, colored liquid. When the light of the lava lamp is turned on, it heats wax collected in the bottom of the lamp. The wax forms a shape which rises to the top of the lamp. There it cools, disperses, and slowly falls back to the bottom. Then it forms a new shape. Each shape is different from the rest, blending from one form into the next.

"The lava lamp illustrates the life cycle of anything that lives in our world. Living things emerge out of the same essence, which is represented by the colored liquid in the lamp. Each being is unique, just as each shape in the liquid has its own form. But it is still of the same liquid. Everything in life comes from Unity and returns back to it.

"The heat from the light bulb in the lamp causing the shapes to form is analogous to the impulse for life that brings spirit into matter in the first place.

"Unity can be experienced in many different ways. One common way is through love and happiness. This usually results from enjoying the feeling of oneness with another. You may not consciously think about it when you are happy. But when you are laughing and taking pleasure in someone's company, you are experiencing a compatibility and rapport with the other person as if the two of you were one.

"Can any of you give me an example from your own life that is an expression of the field of Unity?"

EXPRESSIONS OF UNITY

"The other day," Anne offered, "Jim and I found ourselves driving next to one another on the freeway as we were going home. When we came to our exit, he slowed down to let me merge in front of him. Now, I would expect my husband to do that for me, but not everyone lets you change lanes easily when traffic is heavy."

"I agree," I said. "When you extend a kindness to someone you don't know, it is a wider expression of Unity. Anyone else?"

Don suggested another example. "How about when you warn someone of danger or help a person in need?"

"Yes, those are times when you are essentially 'one' with the other person," I said. "You help him as you would want to be helped."

Lisa remarked, "When you listen to someone who needs to talk out the problems he or she is having, you make a connection on an intuitive level. You really understand the frustration and hardship. You feel as if you are experiencing the same thing. Is this another example of Unity?"

"Yes, it is. Anyone else?" I asked.

"I can't believe it when it happens," Jim offered, "but sometimes it seems that Anne can read my mind. She seems to know what I am thinking. I can't think of an example right now, but she will come up with the same thought that was just on my mind. She knows me very well."

"That used to happen to me and my daughters," said Jane.

"These are all good illustrations of the connections you make with others that are an expression of the field of Unity," I said. "It is beautifully expressed by British writer and orator Annie Besant:

"O, Hidden Life, vibrant in every atom.
"O, Hidden Light, shining in every creature.
"O, Hidden Love, embracing all in Oneness.
"May all who feel themselves at one with thee,
"Know they are therefore one with every other.[1]

"The Oneness of life is also the basis of your laughter when a comedian entertains you about various facets of relationships. The comedian may exaggerate, but the reason you laugh is because there is a truth to what he is saying. You can relate to it and see it in yourself. When he speaks of some of your idiosyncratic behaviors as if they were universal, you feel a sense of unity with him and everyone in the audience. This only makes the subject funnier."

"I think Unity is also demonstrated in the love you give your pet," Jane observed. "Then it responds with a similar kind of love in its devotion back to you.

"Isn't it the same when you cultivate a garden?" wondered Jim. "You show love when you take care of your plants. It is just expressed in a different way."

"I like that idea," agreed Al.

"Is sex an expression of unity?" Lisa asked.

"Yes, it can be," I said. "On the physical plane, sexual union is an expression of Unity in that it provides for a physical joining of the male and female. In a sense, they become one. The physical closeness of sex allows a chance for each person to give pleasure to the other, as well as provide offspring for humanity as a whole.

"Sex is also used as a method for love to be shared through touch, talking, and deeper levels of intuitive communication.

"The urge for a man and a woman to unite with one another is demonstrated not only through the sex drive, but also through the desire to live together and form a family unit. Notice the word 'unit' is contained in the word 'unity.'

"As we have discussed, men and women are complementary. They are automatically attracted to each other to merge and feel whole. Each characteristic that one sex generally holds is balanced by a corresponding, opposite quality in the other. Together, they round out all the possible traits that an individual can have. As a pair, they are stronger together because they have a balance of both masculine and feminine qualities.

"For example, the strength and physical capabilities of the male is complemented by the intuitive understanding of the female. This creates a close bond between them because each one brings something to the relationship to make it more complete."

"Isn't sex also an instinct?" Lisa asked.

"Yes, it is," I said. "It is built into your 'hard wiring,' so to speak. It is in the cellular memory of your body mind, making the sexual urge a natural function of the body.

"The problems that arise with sex are caused when people are drawn into relationships primarily on the basis of their instinctive attractions. The desire for union can overcome good judgment. People lose their ability to make sensible decisions because they are allowing the urges of the body mind to drive them. Good judgment happens when you make decisions using both your physical attractions as well as the wisdom from your higher mind."

"Speaking of male and female relationships," Don said, "what happens to love when two people argue?"

"If you are arguing with someone close to you, such as a family member, you feel as if the person is against you," I explained. "There is a feeling of non-love and separation. The sense of Unity is not in your experience.

"Unity doesn't cease to exist, however. You just lose your awareness of it because your consciousness is wrapped up in defending yourself. You become immersed in the interests of your personal self. When your differences are worked out, you feel a love connection and the feeling of Unity again, because it was never gone in the first place. You simply forgot because you felt threatened and were focused on preserving your position in the argument.

"What distances you from another is an artificial sense of separation, based primarily on your senses. You see where one person's body ends and another begins. Your hands can feel and touch the distinct shape of each individual person. You know you are the only one who uses your mind in order to think.

"Einstein called this misunderstanding an 'optical delusion' acting as a barrier from remembering the Unity of all. He said, 'A human being is part of the whole called by us the "universe," a part limited in time and space. He experiences himself, his thoughts, and his feelings as something separated from the rest — a kind of optical delusion of consciousness. This delusion is a kind of prison for him, restricting him to his personal desires and to affection for a few persons nearest to him. His task must be to free himself from this prison by widening his circle of compassion to embrace all living creatures and the whole of nature in its beauty.'

"Einstein understood the spiritual connection at the basis of every-thing in the world. He knew the illusion of separateness was limited to the physical plane of manifestation. Intuitively, I'm sure you, too, under-stand the links you have with others. You know in your heart, spiritually, you are one with all.

"In another quote, Einstein referred to this aspect of spiritual con-nectedness when he spoke of the 'field.' His use of the term 'matter' per-tains to the physical world. He said, 'There is no place in this new kind of physics for both the field and matter, for the field is the only reality.' The 'field' is the realm of the higher levels of consciousness of which the spiri-tual Self is a part.

"All people together make humanity. They constitute the whole. No individual is more valuable than another. Each has talents and inner good-ness. The core of each person is the same. It is like gold that is made into gold jewelry. It has no more intrinsic value than gold nuggets. Gold jew-elry only seems more valuable because of people's attitudes about it. Gold is gold. The same is true with humanity. The spirituality within each per-son is a manifestation of the same essence. It truly is gold!

"Gold jewelry can be melted down to make something new. This symbolizes the change in personality that a human being undergoes from one lifetime to the next. It also demonstrates the changing nature of the personality from birth to old age. It can start out at the beginning of life to be one way, then become quite different. With wisdom and under-standing, it can develop and refine itself. On the other hand, the person-ality can become resentful and bitter with life. When this happens, how-ever, it only provides more opportunities for learning in the future.

"In any society, each person has a rightful place. Everyone contrib-utes to the function of the whole. Each is important. It is like the fingers of your hand. They all work together. No one single finger can work alone.

"The poet Rumi expresses the unity of humanity in his poetry:

"I, You, He, She, We.
"In the garden of mystic lovers, these are not true distinctions.[2]

"It is said you should treat others with the same care you give yourself. You don't let your left hand remain dirty without using your right hand to clean it. You care about the cleanliness of your whole body.

"Likewise, you care about your entire family. Let this widen to include all humanity, as well as all animals, plants, and the earth itself. The Native Americans speak of the rivers as their brothers. This attitude recognizes the Oneness of all creation.

"Nothing exists in isolation. All things together form the whole. This is the case whether you are looking at a family, a community, or the entire world. You have a connection with everything."

Al said, "I think of how the problems of war or famine in countries in Africa or Eastern Europe can spread and affect the neighboring countries. They may send aid or help refugees who have been displaced."

"Yes, it can seem like something happening on another continent is out of our realm, but everything that happens in the world affects everything else," I agreed.

"Let's look at another example. When one part of a city is in need, such as a section burdened by poverty and lack of resources, it does not exist in isolation. It affects the rest of the city through crime, drug abuse, and civil unrest."

"I think it is necessary for everyone to work on solving the problems of the world, rather than just leaving people to fend for themselves," Jane proclaimed.

"I'm not sure," Don said. "Are we obligated to take of other people?"

"We should at least try," emphasized Lisa.

"This isn't an easy question to answer," I said. "The important thing is to realize that we do not live in isolation. What others do affects us and, in turn, the way we think and act affects them.

"Just like a community operates as a complete system, your physical body functions as an integrated whole. If one part is not working well, all parts suffer. For example, if your feet hurt, you won't feel comfortable no matter what you do. Likewise, if you are emotionally upset, you won't feel well physically or function your best mentally.

"The interconnectedness is seen even at the subatomic level. Physicist H.P. Stapp described it in a lecture titled "The Physics of Consciousness" as he spoke about the particles within an atom. 'An elementary particle is not an independently existing, unanalyzable entity. It is, in essence, a set of relationships that reach outward to other things.'

"There is an exercise that demonstrates the influence we have on everything around us. In a symbolic way, it illustrates how one part of a system is linked to every other part."

I brought out a long, heavy piece of string with the ends tied together. I spread it out so everyone could hold on to it. It was long enough to reach around the entire group.

"A community is like this circle of string. When one part is under stress, the entire system feels it."

I tugged on my section of string so everyone holding it could feel the tension.

"You can feel the effect when I pull on the string, even if I do it gently.

"Let's experiment a little more. Everyone pull on your part. See how the string becomes taut.

"Now, only three people hold on to the string. When I tug my section, you can feel the effect more dramatically than when several people have it in their hands.

"This is similar to what the world experiences when a large section of the population is in need. There is a greater impact on everyone else. The same is true for your community or your family."

As I gathered up the string, I asked what people thought about the exercise.

"It's a creative way to show the impact one person can have on a group," Al remarked. "It makes me remember how my mother could affect the rest of the family if she wasn't feeling well. The string really demonstrates your point."

"I was surprised how much I could feel the effect on the string if only a slight pressure was exerted," Lisa observed.

Jim asked, "Do you mind if I use this demonstration at my company to illustrate the concept in a work environment?"

"Sure, I'm glad it can be useful," I said.

"Just as negative circumstances are felt by everyone in a community, so, too, are efforts to improve things. The effects of positive interventions to those in need extend outward to an even larger area."

"That's a good point," agreed Jim. "It lifts my spirits when I watch the news and see aid workers helping a community that is having problems. I feel comforted when people deliver food or supplies to those in need."

"Sure, it warms your heart. In addition, you feel secure in the thought that someone would help you if you were in trouble. The oneness of humanity is experienced when people come together to solve a crisis. For example, everyone pitches in to help during a flood or if a family has a lost child. The global community also unifies as people tackle issues such as preserving the environment.

"The sense of unity in a neighborhood can be destroyed if people are taught to hate others who are different. Racial prejudice and disharmony between religious groups are examples of this.

"Attempts have been made to counteract some of this hatred. A project was launched in which Irish Catholic and Protestant youths were taken on a wilderness expedition where they had to work together as a team to overcome obstacles they encountered. When they depended upon one another, mutual hatred changed to mutual helpfulness. Eventually, the boys lost all sense of separation and developed feelings of camaraderie.

"Martin Luther King led the United States through many changes during the civil rights struggle in the 1950s and '60s. He advocated the use of nonviolence by his followers in campaigns to counteract racism and other prejudice. He said, 'A basic fact that characterizes nonviolence is that it does not seek to defeat or humiliate the opponent, but to win his friendship and understanding.'[3]

"The use of nonviolent demonstrations to bring about social change is an example of the application of the principle of Unity. It shows respect for the people whom the demonstration is trying to affect. Violence only brings about more separation and hatred.

"Through evolution, all people will gradually come to know and live with the awareness of the interconnectedness of all things. You are aware of it in little ways already. Consider how you feel when someone you love, such as a sister or your mother, receives an achievement award. You feel as happy for her as you would if you had won the award yourself — maybe even more so.

"Take another example. Suppose you and your daughter are driving separate cars and looking for parking places. If you find a spot, you may happily relinquish it to your daughter. You are glad to know that she is secure with parking for that day.

"These examples can be widened to encompass a large group of people. When your nation's team in the Olympics wins a gold medal, you feel a sense of unity with others across the country.

"In life, problems arise when you lose the awareness of unity. In an argument, the differences can seem insurmountable if you look at them only from your viewpoint. If, on the other hand, you 'put yourself in the other's shoes' to understand why he feels as he does, solutions are more easily found.

"In any disagreement, however, it is still important for you to represent your position. Even if you are acting from the realization of unity, you don't necessarily have to give up what you want. There may be a solution you can find so both sides will be able to get their needs met.

"This is called a Win/Win solution. Each side comes out feeling like a winner. This is better than the Win/Lose solution, where only one person comes out feeling like he or she has won. The one who loses is left with feelings of unfairness and inequality.

"The principle of unity can be found in all religions of the world. It is a universal concept. Each philosophy has its own way of presenting it, but they all teach the same basic truths. Every religion appeals to different people depending upon their temperaments. One point of view is like a single slice of pie. All the religious groups together make up the entire pie. Together, they make our understanding more complete, with no one particular philosophy being more right than any other.

"The following analogy illustrates this. Imagine one person looking at an object. He sees a square. Another looks at the same object and sees a circle. If they both trust the vision of the other to increase their understanding, they come to realize that they are looking at a cylinder.

"This is also demonstrated by another example. Imagine that three people are blindfolded and taken to separate parts of an elephant. They are asked to reach out their hands and describe what they think the animal looks like. One may touch the side of the elephant and think he is as large as a house. Another may hold the elephant's trunk and conclude the animal is like a snake. A third may touch the elephant's tusk and think the animal might have a shell. Each is right from his viewpoint. Yet they need each other to get the total picture.

"This is true with anything in life. No one viewpoint gives the whole perspective. Each is valuable. It is summed up in the saying 'From no two mountains do you get the same view.'

"I'd like to share another example that clearly expresses unity. It took place during the Special Olympics in Seattle one year. As you probably know, the Special Olympics is made up of a series of athletic competitions for children who have physical disabilities.

"Nine children were ready to run a foot race. The starting gun was fired, and the children began to sprint. Right away, one child stumbled and fell. He started crying. The other eight children speeding forward heard the cries and stopped. They all came back to help. One bent down and kissed the injured child. Two other children helped him stand up. Then all nine linked their arms together and crossed the finish line as a group. The crowd, in admiration for the compassion shown by the contestants, stood up and applauded. Their cheering lasted for ten minutes."

Lisa expressed amazement, saying, "I can't believe how wonderful that story is. It chokes me up to hear it."

"Me, too," I said. "I have another example of unity, only this time it expresses the harmony that exists in nature. It was written by Ted Perry and adapted from a speech given in 1854 by Chief Sealth, or Seattle, of the Suquamish Indian Tribe. In Chief Sealth's speech, he was responding to the interest the President of the United States had in purchasing land from the Native Americans. Here are some excerpts.

> ". . . the Great Chief in Washington sends word that he wishes to buy our land. . . . If we sell our land, you must remember, and teach your children, that the rivers are our brothers, and yours, and you must henceforth give the rivers the kindness you would give to any brother. . . . The air is precious to the red man, for all things share the same breath-the beasts, the trees, and man, they are all of the same breath. . . . All things are connected. Whatever befalls the earth, befalls the sons and daughters of

the earth. Man did not weave the web of life; he is merely
a strand in it. Whatever he does to the web, he does to
himself. . . . How can you buy or sell the sky, the warmth
of the land, the swiftness of the antelope? The idea is
strange to us. . . . If we do not own the freshness of the
air and the sparkle of the water, how can you buy them
from us?[4]

"One of the texts of ancient Buddhist literature, the Dhammapada,
also instructs us to live in harmony with nature and all human beings. In
verse 3:10, it speaks of a wise man who earns his living without harming
anything he comes in contact with.

"The wise and moral man
"Shines like a fire on a hilltop,
"Making money like the bee
"Who does not hurt the flower.

"William Blake, the English poet, understood the unity of all. He
expressed it when he wrote in Auguries of Innocence:

"To see a world in a grain of sand
"And a heaven in a wild flower,
"Hold infinity in the palm of your hand
"And eternity in an hour."

THE SOURCE

"As you already know, the highest plane of consciousness is the field
of Unity. This is the field from which all things in the manifested world
emerge. However, it is easy to wonder whether there is another field 'higher'
than it, or where this field comes from.

"First of all, there is no other level of consciousness above it. The field
of Unity is the plane where all manifestation is one. But you might ask,
what gives rise to it in the first place? What causes it? Intuitively, it makes
sense that 'something' is behind the impulse for life. But what is it?

"Unfortunately, the answer to that question is unexplainable in everyday language. Only through your intuition can you grasp a sense of it. It is like trying to describe where the wind comes from."

"I like your analogy," said Al. "I can't say why, but I know what you are talking about."

"That's exactly what I mean," I said. "The reason you comprehend this is because, at a deep level, you know you are part of this mysterious 'something.' You intuitively recognize it because it is at the core of your being. It is the Divine Spark within you. It is in all things in the physical world. Just as a river with its many branches has its source in the mountains, everything around us has its source in the Divine.

"This mysterious 'something' has been called various names by different traditions. In the Christian and Jewish tradition, it is called God. In Islam, it is called Allah. In Hinduism, it is Brahman or Parabrahman, and in Chinese Taoism, it is the Tao (pronounced 'dou' as in 'doubt').

"Zoroastrianism is the religion from the teacher Zoroaster where the primordial source is called Ahura Mazda. The mystics of Islam, the Sufis, have referred to it as 'the breath inside the breath.' In the Jewish tradition, it is known as Yahweh, Jehovah, or Hashem. The Native American Dakota tribe uses the term Wakan Tanka. It is also called the Supreme, the Source, the Creator, Be-ness, and the Divine.

"Many words may be used to refer to the power of God or the Supreme, but all are inadequate to convey its character. To describe it by listing its qualities is also insufficient. They are innumerable. The Source is ungraspable, unfathomable, and unknowable. It is before time and space. In the words of Helena Blavatsky in *The Secret Doctrine*, it is 'eternal, invisible, yet Omnipresent, without beginning or end, yet periodical in regular manifestations, . . . unconscious, yet absolute Consciousness; unrealizable, yet the one self-existing reality. . . .'[5]

"God, or the Supreme, is not conscious. It is not a separate consciousness that perceives you or the world. Out of it, consciousness is created. Consciousness can be thought of as the 'body' of the Supreme.

"A saying from the Ancient Wisdom refers to the Supreme as a 'sphere with its center everywhere and its circumference nowhere.' "

"That's quite a deep concept," Al said.

"Yes, it is. That metaphor speaks to the grandness and pervasiveness of the Supreme. God is unseen. It is like daylight that makes everything visible while it remains invisible. A ray of light is not seen unless intercepted by specks of dust. The Supreme makes everything known, but remains unknown itself.

"This is described in the Koran 6.103: 'No vision can grasp him, but His grasp is over all vision. He is above all comprehension, yet is acquainted with all things.'

"God cannot be perceived at the mental level. God is beyond the mind. It is what makes perception possible. God is the power that moves the universe, yet it is the same power that moves you to eat, drink, and sleep.

"The Supreme cannot be found anywhere. It is not of a nature to be found. Nothing can contain it. It is what contains everything else.

"It does not manifest as itself. It is only known by the many things in which it is manifested, ranging from spiritual essence down to physical form.

"It is written in the Hermetica, an Egyptian scripture attributed to the ancient sage Hermes Trimegistus, that God is 'hidden, yet obvious everywhere . . . . He is bodiless, yet embodied in everything. . . . He is the unity in all things.'

"The same idea is expressed in the following Hindu metaphor, 'Just as a tree is contained in a single seed, and butter pervades milk, the Source is in everything.'

"Nothing can affect the Supreme. Nothing that happens on the physical plane affects God. Just as the beginning of a river is not affected by the whirlpools and rapids within, the Source is not changed by anything that you do, feel, or think. The Source is like a well, used but never used up.

"Some may disbelieve or doubt the existence of God because nothing about God can be proven. God is unseen. Its existence is accepted intuitively. Some would say if you can't see God, then God doesn't exist. But this defies the reasoning of one argument that makes its point in this way.

"You have a friend, but you don't know your friend's mother. Just because you haven't met her or seen her, you cannot say that the mother doesn't exist. Your friend's existence implies the presence of a mother. So, too, the presence of everything in our world implies the existence of God.

"Every person perceives God in his own way. It is like a woman who can be a mother to her children, a sister to her brother, a wife to her husband, and a daughter to her father. No matter how she appears, she is still one and the same, as the Source is only One.

"Martin Luther King spoke of the existence of God when he said, 'I am convinced that the universe is under the control of a loving purpose, and that in the struggle for righteousness man has cosmic companionship. Behind the harsh appearance of the world there is a benign power.'[6] King understood that human beings must grow and evolve, sometime from struggles and hardships. He understood the purpose of it and sensed the guidance of a Divine Presence.

"Einstein also spoke about the existence of a supreme Source when he wrote, 'Everyone who is seriously involved in the pursuit of science becomes convinced that a Spirit is manifest in the Laws of the Universe — a Spirit vastly superior to that of man, and one in the face of which we, with our modest powers, must feel humble.'

"These quotes and metaphors give you an idea of the wide variety of ways the Source has been described. The subject is too big for words. Each person can only begin to grasp it in a limited way through his or her intuition.

"Now, before we delve into the treats we brought for our last class session, let us take a few minutes for a final meditation.

"Because we started today's class with the influence of Buddhism as we 'adjusted our motivation,' I'd like to end the class in a similar way. A tradition Buddhists may use is to end a gathering by 'dedicating' the value they received from the teaching to all living beings. This means that whatever is gained will be thought of not only as a benefit for the individual himself, but also for everyone else who lives in the world.

"So, let us relax and get into a comfortable position to meditate for a few minutes.

"Let us feel harmony as a group.

"Let us feel harmony with nature.

"Think of a moment of inspiration you have experienced. Bring that moment into the your awareness.

"Be a part of the peace within you. Realize you are that peace.

"Experience the silence within.

"Focus your attention within your heart. Open to the love within and send that love to those you know who need it.

"Let us send peace and good will to the community, the nation, and the world.

"Finally, let us conclude with the influence of Buddhism as we 'adjust our motivation.' Let us dedicate the value we have received from all the classes to every being who lives in this world."

NOTES

1. Joy Mills, "O Hidden Life," *The Theosophist*, June 1976.
2. Quoted from a video of Coleman Barks, translator, reciting poems of Jalaluddin Rumi.
3. Coretta Scott King et al., *The Martin Luther King, Jr., Companion* (New York: St. Martin's Press, 1993), p. 43.
4. Eli Gifford and R. Michael Cook, eds., *How Can One Sell the Air?: Chief Seattle's Vision* (Summertown, Tennessee: The Book Publishing Company, 1992), pp. 32, 35, 41, 47, and 48.
5. Helena Petrovna Blavatsky, *The Secret Doctrine*, Vol. I (Pasadena, California: Theosophical University Press, 1963), p. 2.
6. King, pp. 51 and 52.